W9-BUE-895

OVID

METAMORPHOSES XI

OVID

METAMORPHOSES XI

Edited with Introduction,
Commentary and Vocabulary by
G.M.H. MURPHY

Bristol Classical Press

This impression 2003
This edition published in 1991 by
Bristol Classical Press
an imprint of
Gerald Duckworth & Co. Ltd.
90-93 Cowcross Street, London EC1M 6BF
Tel: 020 7490 7300
Fax: 020 7490 0080
inquiries@duckworth-publishers.co.uk
www.ducknet.co.uk

First published in 1972 by Oxford University Press

© 1972 by Oxford University Press

A catalogue record for this book is available
from the British Library

ISBN 0 906515 40 8

PREFACE

In writing the introduction and commentary to this edition I have tried to keep in mind those students of Latin literature at sixth-form and undergraduate level who may not be classical specialists and who need to be helped towards an appreciation of Ovid as a literary artist.

The text is based on that of Rudolf Ehwald (Teubner, 1915). Divergences from the Teubner text are noted in the commentary, and the disputed passages are summarised in Appendix I. I have derived much help from the previous Clarendon Press edition by G. A. T. Davies (1907) and from the Haupt-Ehwald commentary revised by von Albrecht.

I wish to acknowledge my indebtedness to B. G. Teubner Verlag, Stuttgart, for permission to use the Ehwald text; to the Macmillan Company of New York for permission to reproduce an extract from Arthur Golding's translation of *Metamorphoses* edited by J. F. Nims (1965), and to Indiana University Press for permission to include an extract from *Metamorphoses* translated by Rolfe Humphries (1955).

I owe a particular debt of gratitude to Mr A. S. Hollis, who read the whole of the manuscript and helpfully suggested many new lines of approach. He has been very generous with his scholarship. The manuscript also benefited greatly at an earlier stage from the vigilant and trenchant criticism of Mr A. H. C. Griffin. I am grateful to Mr A. G. Lee for his invaluable advice on some problems of the text, and to Mr R. D. Williams.

G. M. H. MURPHY

CONTENTS

INTRODUCTION

OVID, THE MAN AND THE WRITER

Publius Ovidius Naso, the least 'Augustan' of the Augustan poets, was born in 43 B.C., the year after Caesar's murder, in the town of Sulmo, some eighty miles east of Rome. His father, an established equestrian, sent the boy to be educated with his brother at Rome. The education which the two boys received was predominantly rhetorical, and the training in debating technique and verbal facility was to leave a lasting mark on the young poet's mind. After a period of study in Athens and of travel in Asia Minor, Ovid returned to Rome to begin the political career which was his father's ambition for him, but it was not long before he abandoned politics for the poetry which was his first love. In a brief autobiographical sketch (*Tristia* iv. 10) he tells us that even as a boy, verse was his second nature.[1] Now as a young man he began to give public recitations of his poems, and it was not long before he became the most fashionable poet of his time.

Aged only 13 in the year of the battle of Actium, Ovid was not old enough to have experienced the worst evils of civil war, and therefore he did not have the same reason as older writers such as Vergil and Horace to appreciate the benefits of the Augustan settlement. If Ovid avoided the grand political theme it was also simply because he was not a political animal; his interests led him to concern himself rather with the private, more intimate life of pleasure and love. (To point out these differences is not to

[1] sponte sua carmen numeros veniebat ad aptos,
   et quod temptabam dicere versus erat.   (*Tristia* iv. 10, 25–6)

make invidious comparisons between Ovid and, say, Vergil
or Horace; it is to try to define Ovid's particularity). We
find in his poems none of that scathing denunciation of
contemporary life, none of that praise of lost simplicity and
rustic virtue which is so frequent a theme in Roman
literature. Ovid loved the sophisticated pleasures of urban
life and metropolitan culture, and – what was more
startling – he said so:

> prisca iuvent alios; ego me nunc denique natum
>   gratulor; haec aetas moribus apta meis.
>
> (Ars Amatoria iii. 121–2)

He liked modern life, he said, not because of the new material
improvements and discoveries, but because above all it was
more cultured ('quia cultus adest'). This love of refinement,
elegance and polish, so evident in all his poems, gives us a key
to the poet's own character. The elder Seneca (*Controversiae* ii.
2, 8) tells us that he was a man of good character and equable
temperament which made him well loved ('habebat ille
comptum et decens et amabile ingenium'). Ovid himself
tells us of his easy-going and lazy nature (*Amores* i. 9, 41)
and speaks of the serenity of mind (*Tristia*, i. 1, 39) necessary
for poetic creation.[1] These and other hints add up to the
picture of a man at peace with the world, at home in society
and in love with beauty. He was married three times, and
the last of these marriages was both happy and long. This
was the man – a lover of home and city life, sociable,
cultivated and genial – who in A.D. 8, at the age of fifty,
was suddenly relegated by the emperor and sent to spend
his last years in exile on the remote Black Sea coast. To a
man of Ovid's temperament the blow must have been
crushing, and it is hardly surprising that in his last letters
from exile he falls prey to self-pity. The real reasons for

---

[1] Cf. ibid. v. 12, 3–4:

> carmina laetum
> sunt opus, et pacem mentis habere volunt.

Augustus' sentence may never be known. Ovid himself (*Tristia* ii. 207) names them as 'carmen et error'. The offending poem was almost certainly the *Ars Amatoria*, written eight years before, a poem whose moral flippancy ran counter to that spirit of moral 'gravitas' which Augustus sought to revive in Roman society. As for the 'error', the most likely conjecture is that Ovid had accidentally witnessed some crime in which a member of the imperial family was involved, and for this reason had to be removed. Though the circumstances of Ovid's exile were not punitive (he retained his freedom and his property), the choice of so remote a spot as Tomi (now Constanza in Rumania) was unprecedented, and reveals the extent of Augustus' displeasure. Ovid remained in Tomi until his death in A.D. 17, outliving Augustus by three years.

Ovid excelled above all in elegiac poetry, and made the elegiac couplet an instrument of witty love poetry. In the *Amores*, originally written in 16 B.C., and later abbreviated to three books, love is treated for the first time as a literary game. The poet's love for his 'Corinna' is no tempestuous passion: what gives the poems their special flavour is a cool, detached self-mockery. The same element of play is to be found in the *Heroides*, imaginary letters in elegiac form, written by mythological heroines to their absent or unfaithful husbands or lovers. The genre was Ovid's own invention, though he may have derived the idea from Propertius' Arethusa letter (iv. 3). The medium allowed him to put his rhetorical training to good use: in imagining what a heroine would have said in given circumstances, he could draw on his command of the 'suasoria', that rhetorical exercise in which the pupil, presented with a real historical situation (Hannibal before the Alps, for instance) was required to marshal the arguments for or against a particular course of action. Like much of Ovid's poetry, the *Heroides* is at one remove away from reality: the heroines have the air of actresses going through their histrionic motions.

Ovidian wit could also take the form of parody, as in the *Ars Amatoria*, published soon after 1 B.C., a parody of the didactic form in which the subject is not agriculture or astronomy but how to win a girl's favours in modern Rome. It is the incongruity between the solemnity of the genre and the flippancy of the subject-matter which makes for much of the comedy, though these literary considerations doubtless did not mollify Augustus to whom it must have seemed morally insidious.[1] It was followed by other didactic parodies; *de Medicamine Faciei*, on the subject of cosmetics, and the *Remedia Amoris*, a sequel to the *Ars*, published before A.D. 2. The *Metamorphoses* was written between 2 and 8 A.D. and was still in an unfinished state when Ovid left for exile. Another work interrupted by banishment was the *Fasti*, a calendar of the Roman year, filled with antiquarian and religious lore; of this only six books survive, those covering the first six months of the year. The years of exile produced two works of epistolary verse: the *Tristia* and the *Epistolae ex Ponto*. To this list should be added the *Ibis*, a long poem of imprecation against a private enemy of the poet, and one work which the critic Quintilian rated above all the rest but which has not survived – the tragedy *Medea*. 'It seems to me to show', he says, in the tones of the school report, 'how much Ovid could have achieved if he had chosen to direct his talent rather than indulge it' (*Institutiones Oratoriae* x. 1, 98). There is no doubt that Ovid was a master of the dramatic monologue; that is clear from a reading of such speeches as those of Myrrha (*Met.* x. 319ff.), Byblis (*Met.* ix. 474ff.) and Medea (*Met.* vii. 11ff.).

[1] Later, from exile, Ovid pleaded that the book had been written in a spirit of irony and that he did not necessarily condone what he described:

>   crede mihi, distant mores a carmine nostro.
>   vita verecunda est, Musa iocosa mea,
>   magnaque pars mendax operum est et ficta meorum:
>   plus sibi permisit compositore suo.   (*Tristia*, ii. 353–6)

By then, however, it was too late to teach Augustus a literary lesson.

However the psychological perception revealed in these speeches is only one aspect of Ovid's many-sided genius.

THE METAMORPHOSES

The *Metamorphoses* was Ovid's only poem in epic form. It belongs to the Hesiodic rather than the Homeric tradition of epic, that is to say it does not narrate one continuous story like the Iliad or the Odyssey, it is, like Hesiod's *Theogony*, a collection of stories linked by a single theme which is common to all. Ovid's choice of theme – change of shape – was particularly felicitous, for it is a theme which runs through the folklore of all ages, from Circe's pigs to Cinderella's pumpkins and beyond. Such stories are often attached to natural phenomena such as rocks and trees whose features resemble human or animal shapes and which for that reason are said once to have been animals or humans. A Greek collection of metamorphosis stories, the *Heteroioumena*, was written in the second century B.C. by Nicander of Colophon, and earlier there had been the *Ornithogonia* by the Hellenistic poet Boeus or Boeo, a collection of bird transformation stories, and Eratosthenes' *Catasterismoi*, metamorphoses into stars. Nearer Ovid's own day was Parthenius of Nicea, who taught in Rome *c.* 54 B.C. and wrote a poem called the *Metamorphoses*. Ovid undoubtedly drew on some, if not all of these precursors (Boeo's work had been turned into Latin by his friend Aemilius Macer), but unlike some of them he does not treat his theme subject by subject (rocks, birds, trees, stars, etc.) but chronologically, from the creation of the world to the present day (that is to say the age of Augustus).[1] After the account of the origins of human life in Book i, we move on to the stories of the gods, then to

[1] The 'chronological' sequence, however, is of the vaguest. Some of the 'timeless' myths are inserted where they will provide variation or contrast; thus the Narcissus story (*Met.* iii. 339–510) is placed in the middle of the Theban cycle.

the heroic age, and finally at the end of Book xv to historical times.

In many of these stories the actual metamorphosis plays only a small part, and sometimes it is difficult to find any metamorphosis at all. Yet as a unifying theme for a 'perpetuum carmen' (*Met.* i. 4) it is well chosen. No poet was better fitted to sing of change than the Protean Ovid, the conjuror with words, the master of variety. The form is perfectly suited to the matter. Everything in the *Metamorphoses* is constantly changing: there is a constant alteration and variation of mood, of place, of characters, of standpoint – not only from one story to another but within the same story. Ovid had neither the need nor the inclination to justify his love of variety by appealing to philosophy, but in the fifteenth book, in a long passage concerned with the teachings of the Greek philosopher Pythagoras, he shows that nothing is immune to change ('nihil est toto, quod perstet, in orbe', *Met.* xv. 177). Even the present moment does not exist, for a new moment is forever taking its place:

Tempora sic fugiunt pariter, pariterque sequuntur
et nova sunt semper; nam quod fuit ante relictum est
fitque quod haud fuerat, momentaque cuncta novantur.
(ibid. 183–5)

Ovid does not pursue this Pythagoreanism, but nevertheless the fact that he states the philosophy shows perhaps that he was aware of a deeper link between his stories than mere coincidence.

The *Metamorphoses*, then, is a collection of separate stories linked by their common theme and epic form. For the short miniature narratives, Ovid's model was the epyllion, a literary form developed by the Hellenistic poets of Alexandria such as Callimachus and Theocritus. The Alexandrians, with their fastidious literary taste, favoured the small-scale filigree poem, and shunned the grand scale. The epyllion was a narrative poem of moderate length, including some speech and, at some point, a digression or miniature inset. The *Hecale* of Callimachus was the best known example of the genre, which by Ovid's time already had its Latin imitators; Licinius Calvus had written an *Io*, and Cicero a *Halcyones*. Another characteristic of the epyllion was the *ekphrasis* – a detailed piece of descriptive scene-painting in which every detail was outlined with exquisite elaboration. All these characteristic features of the epyllion are to be found in *Met.* xi, in the Ceyx and Alcyone story. But what makes the *Metamorphoses* unique is that this small-scale Alexandrian elegance is married to the large-scale epic form. The elegiac form, which had been Ovid's chosen medium hitherto, was well suited to the expression of elegant variations on a love theme, but a continuous, flowing narrative could only be expressed in epic hexameters. Ovid shows a complete mastery of epic technique. He was, of course, able to benefit from the example and experience of Vergil. Brooks Otis, in his book *Ovid as an epic poet*, has shown how Ovid adapted Vergil's style to his own purposes, particularly in the way he identifies himself with his characters and enters emotionally into the narrative. However it would be a mistake to imagine that Ovid in any way sought to rival Vergil. All the parts of the Aeneid are subservient to one dominant theme, the theme of Rome's destiny; no single episode is allowed to assume a disproportionate importance, lest this overall theme be obscured. This proportion is lacking in Ovid, who develops each episode of the *Metamorphoses*, and the separate details within each episode, for its own sake. Secondly, the sense of religious mystery, so powerful in Vergil, is alien to Ovid. It is characteristic that in his account of the return of Aeneas and the Sybil from the underworld Ovid should picture them as seeking distraction from the journey in casual conversation.

> cum duce Cumaea mollit sermone laborem
>
> (*Met.* xiv. 121)

It is hard to imagine Vergil's Sybil passing the time of day in idle gossip! All Ovid's characters are, like their author, brilliantly articulate. They are also, for epic, notably un-heroic. There are, it is true, conventional battle-scenes, like the fight between Lapiths and Centaurs in *Met.* xii, but these are uninteresting exercises where Ovid is simply displaying his command of the genre and showing that he can outdo his predecessors in the bloodthirstiness of the detail.[1] It is the unheroic heroes who are more memorable – Acis, for instance, who, faced with the angry Cyclops, does not stand his ground like a David before Goliath but runs, calling on his girl-friend and parents to help him (*Met.* xiii. 879–81).

The *Metamorphoses*, in short, is not serious epic, to be considered on the same level as the Aeneid: it is a kind of play upon epic. This play takes many forms, ranging from wit and humour to the kind of literary exercise mentioned above. Humour is absent only at the beginning of the work (the magnificent account of Chaos changing into Cosmos), and at the end (where this change is repeated on the political scale, as Augustus brings civil order out of civil chaos). Elsewhere, humour is never far below the surface, and it is usually based on some form of incongruity. The whole point about the 'divine comedy' which begins at i. 452 is that the gods are seen to behave in a most ungodlike way. Love and dignity do not go together:

> Non bene conveniunt, nec in una sede morantur
> maiestas et amor.   (ii. 846–7)

Love in the *Metamorphoses* is the great leveller, reducing goddesses to nagging shrews and gods to absurd old roués. The follies and selfish vanities of the gods are really the

[1] The horrific or bloodthirsty passages in the *Metamorphoses* (see especially the Philomela story in Book vi) satisfied a taste for *Grand Guignol* inherited from Alexandrian literature. Urban and sedentary cultures often develop a need for this kind of vicarious excitement.

follies and vanities of contemporary Roman society, distorted and magnified. Just as Offenbach's mythological characters (in *Orpheus in the Underworld* and *La Belle Hélène*) represent the *haute bourgeoisie* of Second Empire Paris in fancy dress, so Ovid burlesques the society of his day by peopling Olympus with his contemporaries.

There is incongruity, too, in Ovid's use of imagery. He loves the jarring image, often drawn from everyday life. When, for instance, Pyramus stabs himself on discovering Thisbe's torn veil, who but Ovid would have compared the spurting blood to a jet of water from a burst water main?

> cruor emicat alte
> non aliter quam cum vitiato fistula plumbo
> scinditur et tenui stridente foramine longas
> eiaculatur aquas.   (iv. 121–4)

There is another example of such engaging anachronism in iii. 111–14, when Cadmus sows the dragon's teeth in the ground: the warriors, Ovid says, emerged from the ground like the figures on a theatre-curtain (Roman curtains were pulled up from below, not dropped). The incongruity may also be a matter of style, as in xi. 352–78, when Peleus' rustic cowherd delivers his urgent message with all the circumlocutions of the high epic style, including an elaborate description of the scenery. Sometimes it is the situation which is incongruous, as when Perseus, with the sea-monster already advancing upon the terror-stricken Andromeda, politely introduces himself to her parents and finds time, by modestly listing his exploits and pedigree, to strike a hard marriage-bargain (iv. 694–702). There is incongruity, too, in the twist Ovid gives a story already well-known in another version. Vergil, for instance, in his version of the Orpheus and Eurydice legend (Georgics iv. 457–527) portrays Pluto as a remote and dreadful monarch beyond Orpheus' reach. Not so Ovid, who shows us an almost impudent Orpheus, not in the least awed by his surroundings. 'I have not come here to see the sights', he tells Pluto in effect ('non huc, ut opaca viderem Tartara, descendi', x. 20–1): 'Love brought me here. He is a god well-known on earth, and I fancy not unknown down here, if the stories about you are correct':

> supera deus hic bene notus in ora est;
> an sit et hic dubito: sed et hic tamen auguror esse,
> famaque si veteris non est mentita rapinae,
> vos quoque iunxit Amor   (ibid. 26–9)

Humour, then, what Cicero calls 'perpetua festivitas' or 'perpetuae facetiae', (de Oratore ii. 219, 243) pervades the Metamorphoses. In addition, there is verbal wit (what he calls 'dicacitas'; 'peracutum ac breve, quod in celeritate atque dicto est'). Puns, double meanings, paradoxes – the poem is spiced with every kind of verbal trick. Ovid relishes dexterity for its own sake. How else are we to explain a line such as this, from the Tristia (i. 1, 18):

> Si quis qui quid agam forte requirat erit?

He is particularly fond of playing upon the double aspect of metamorphosis itself, or of distinguishing the personal and abstract attributes of a god only to confuse them later with the ambiguity of a pronoun. When Io, for instance, changed into a cow, sees her reflection in the water, she 'runs away from herself' ('seque exsternata refugit', Met. i. 641). The sun god, in mourning for his son Phaeton, 'shuns himself' ('lucemque odit seque ipse diemque', ii. 383). When the god of sleep awakes from sleep he 'shakes himself off himself' ('excussit . . . sibi se', xi. 621). Sometimes the conventions of epic diction are strained to breaking point. When Midas, who has received the gift of the golden touch from Bacchus, mixes wine with water, he 'mixes his benefactor' ('miscuerat puris auctorem muneris undis', xi. 125). In this last case Ovid is giving a further twist to the convention whereby the god's name was used to denote his product. Again, parallelisms are used, sometimes for their own sake and sometimes for special effect, as in xi. 517-18:

> inque fretum credas totum descendere caelum,
> inque plagas caeli tumefactum adscendere pontum.

In these lines, the almost word for word similarity of pattern and consonantal sound, together with the end rhyme, emphasises the merging confusion of sea and sky. Ovid's wit extends to the *double entendre*, as in Narcissus' cry 'Coeamus!' – so misinterpreted by Echo (iii. 386). Sometimes the epic catalogue is parodied, as at iii. 206-24, where the names of all thirty of Actaeon's hounds are listed, or at xiii. 789-807, where Polyphemus describes the charms of Galatea with a succession of no less then twenty-nine similes.

This dexterity, this love of pyrotechnical display, has won for Ovid the rebukes of critics both ancient and modern. 'Cleverness' was the term most often applied to him by the ancient critics – and that has always been an ambiguous word. Quintilian saw him as 'too much enamoured of his own cleverness' ('nimium amator ingenii sui' – x. 1, 88). Sixteen hundred years later Dryden elaborated the charge in his *Preface to Fables Ancient and Modern*: 'The Vulgar Judges, which are Nine Parts in Ten of all Nations, who call Conceits and Jingles Wit, who see *Ovid* full of them, and *Chaucer* altogether without them, will think me little less than mad for preferring the *Englishman* to the *Roman*: Yet, with their leave, I must presume to say, that the things they admire are only glittering *Trifles*, and so far from being Witty, that in a serious poem they are nauseous, because they are unnatural. Wou'd any Man who is ready to die for Love, describe his Passion like *Narcissus*? Wou'd he think of *inopem me copia fecit*, and a dozen more of such expressions, pour'd on the neck of one another, and signifying all the same Thing? . . . On these occasions the Poet shou'd endeavour to raise Pity; but instead of this, *Ovid* is tickling you to laugh'.

'In a serious poem': here is the crux. Dryden's criticism starts from a false premiss, because while the *Metamorphoses* does contain straightforwardly serious passages, it is basically a comedy, perhaps the most subtle work of comic genius written in Latin. It is a poem whose immediate subject is not life, but art; the scenery is stage scenery, and the heroes and heroines are actors and actresses. It is absurd to consider the *Metamorphoses* on a par with the *Aeneid* and then to call it a 'flawed epic'. Ceyx and Alcyone, for instance (in Book xi) are more convincingly characterised than most of Ovid's heroes and heroines but they cannot stand comparison with, say, Dido and Aeneas; the very notion is absurd, and to treat the episode as a tragedy is to put an intolerable weight on a poem which has other attractions. The same is true of the *Pyramus and Thisbe* story in Book iv which for all its prettiness can hardly be compared with *Romeo and Juliet*. Ovid's star-crossed lovers have neither the depth nor the motivation to engage the reader's emotions.

What the ancient, and some modern, critics objected to in Ovid was really his originality. That he took account of these criticisms and yet rejected them is evident from an anecdote of the elder Seneca, who tells us that some friends of the poet asked to be allowed to choose three lines from his poetry which they thought should have been rejected. Ovid agreed, but on condition that he too be allowed to choose three lines which he would on no account have changed, and when the results were compared the two parties were found to have chosen the same three lines (*Controversiae* ii. 2, 12). Seneca tells us what two of the lines were:

> et gelidum Borean egelidumque Notum
> > (*Amores* ii. 11, 10)

and

> semibovemque virum semivirumque bovem
> > (*Ars Amatoria* ii. 24 – of the Minotaur)

Both exemplify that love of word-play of which Ovid saw
no need to be ashamed. Seneca tells us that he believed a
face was more attractive for having a mole on it ('decentiorem
faciem esse in qua aliquis naevus fuisset'). The difference
is really one of aesthetic taste: Ovid was one of those who
find the perfectly unified and smoothly harmonious work of
art a trifle tedious.

The fact that the *Metamorphoses* has inspired so many
painters is significant. Ovid sees everything – colours,
movements, groupings, poses – with a painter's eye. It is
interesting to look at the way, for instance, he introduces his
description of Thetis' cove (xi. 229–36):

> est specus in medio, natura factus an arte
> ambiguum, magis arte tamen.

The scenery is inspired more by art than by nature, and
indeed many of the features of the landscape of the *Metamorphoses* are to be found in surviving frescoes of the period,
such as those at Pompeii.[1] If much of the Aeneid is bathed
in the dim and mysterious light of antiquity, the stories of
the Metamorphoses are played out in an atmosphere of
clear and brilliant sunlight. The colouring is always
effective, and the word-order often reflects a juxtaposition of
colours, as in ii. 864–5:

> et nunc adludit *viridi*que exsultat in herba,
> nunc latus in *fulvis niveum* deponit harenis.

and i. 112:

> *flava*que de *viridi* stillabant ilice mella.

Ovid excelled, too, in the evocation of cool streams and
crystal pools, perhaps because his own youth was spent in a
part of Italy that abounded in streams and well watered
meadows (cf. *Tristia* iv. 10, 3: 'Sulmo mihi patria est,
gelidis uberrimus undis'). However, in its accumulation of

---

[1] See P. Grimal: 'Les Métamorphoses d'Ovide et la Peinture paysagiste
à l'époque d'Auguste', in *Revue des Études Latines* 1938, pp. 145–61.

exquisite detail and miniaturism, Ovidian landscape owes
less to observed nature than to Alexandrian poetry and the
Hellenistic style of wall painting. Out of these ingredients
Ovid created an ideal landscape that was to serve European
art well.

Although we have stressed the essential artistry of Ovid,
this does not mean that his poetry is remote from real
experience and the deeper concerns of the heart. His sympathetic understanding of the vagaries of human emotion
is best seen in the dramatic monologues of Byblis (*Met.*
ix. 474–563), and Myrrha (*Met.* x. 319–55) – both victims of unnatural passion. He creates a world of happy
endings, where a lover's wish only has to be uttered to
come true. Love makes Pygmalion's statue come to life
(*Met.* x. 294), it turns Iphis into a boy just in time for
Ianthe's wedding (ix. 785–91), and it immortalises the
union of Ceyx and Alcyone (xi. 741–48). The theme of
renunciation is absent: unlike Vergil, Ovid does not
require his lovers to sacrifice their happiness for the sake of a
higher ideal. His ideal is a love that is truly reciprocal, like
that of Cephalus and Procris:

> Coniuge eram felix, felix erat illa marito.
> *Mutua cura* duos et *amor socialis* habebat.
>
> (vii. 799–800)

His pity is reserved for those, like Narcissus, who are
imprisoned by their inability to love anyone but themselves.

It is the private, not the public world that Ovid celebrates,
and it was perhaps this lack of political commitment that
contributed towards his fall. Some passages in the *Metamorphoses* could perhaps have been taken as an indirect
criticism of the Augustan establishment. Literary Romans
were accustomed to making the sophisticated distinction
between the gods who were figures of mythological literature and the gods who were the objects of official worship,
but on the whole Augustan poetry treated the gods with

reverence (Vergil's Jupiter, for instance, is far more of a *god* than Homer's Zeus). Ovid, however, is no respecter of divine persons: his gods are trivial, and they abuse their power for the sake of spite and revenge. There is an eloquent contrast in Book xi. between the pious Alcyone, who comes to pray daily at Juno's shrine, offering sacrifices for the safe return of her husband, and the bored and indifferent goddess who wants to be rid of her. There is in many of the stories a glaring disproportion between human offence and divine punishment: Actaeon is torn to pieces by Diana's hounds for having seen the goddess naked, and Niobe's children are brutally shot down because of a rash boast by their mother. Divine revenge is inspired not by justice but by spite. The effect of passages such as these must have been to cast doubt on the whole facade of Augustan neo-Olympian religion. More straightforwardly comic are the episodes in which Jupiter and his wife are presented as a philanderer and a shrew. They are like the characters of a domestic farce, each watching for the other's next move in the game of deceit. Jupiter is always on the look-out for some new girl to chase, even if it means facing a row when he gets home (ii. 424), while Juno is a hardened detective of her husband's infidelity (i. 601 ff.). Such irreverence towards the supreme figurehead of established religion may well have made Augustus himself – that 'praesens divus' (Horace, *Odes* iii. 5, 2) – feel his own dignity to be endangered.

OVID'S INFLUENCE ON LATER LITERATURE AND ART

Parte tamen meliore mei super alta perennis
astra ferar, nomenque erit indelebile nostrum,
quaque patet domitis Romana potentia terris
ore legar populi, perque omnia saecula fama,
si quid habent veri vatum praesagia, vivam.

(Met. xv. 875–9)

The *Metamorphoses* aptly ends with the word 'vivam'. It is a poem sparkling with life, and it has been a source of life and inspiration to succeeding generations of poets and artists; in this sense we have not seen the last of Ovid's many metamorphoses. When the classical authors were rediscovered by the Christian Middle Ages, it was the more spiritual Vergil who first held sway. Then, in the late eleventh and early twelfth centuries scholars and poets suddenly became aware of Ovid's world of sensuality and wit. Library catalogues of this, the *aetas Ovidiana*, show how popular Ovid's works became, and the poetry of the day is pervaded by an Ovidian scepticism and love of beauty. To resolve the contradiction between Ovid and Christian morality, resort was had to the familiar medieval device of allegory. Already in the twelfth century a French liturgical poem speaks of Christ as the divine Orpheus descending into hell to rescue his bride (the Church) from death:

> Sponsam suam ab inferno
> regno locans in superno
> noster traxit Orpheus![1]

This allegorising reached its climax in the fourteenth century *Ovide Moralisé*, a French translation accompanied by 70,000 lines of moralising commentary in verse. Some parallels were easy to make: Deucalion and Pyrrha, for instance, were 'types' of Noah and his wife, while Phaethon's fall stood for that of Lucifer, but the *Ovide Moralisé* found a spiritual meaning in unexpected details. Even in 1480, the frontispiece of Caxton's *Metamorphoses* could portray Ovid as a monk in his cell, praying for the inspiration of the Holy Spirit.

With the advent of Renaissance humanism, poets, scholars and artists needed no moral justification for their delight in the vividness and sensuousness of Ovidian

---

[1] Quoted by P. Dronke in *The Return of Eurydice, Classica et Medievalia* xxiii (1962).

poetry. The first English verse rendering of the *Metamorphoses* appeared in 1567. Each of the Elizabethans derived something different from his reading of Ovid: if in Spenser the influence made for sweetness and musicality (Spenser read his Ovid through the eyes of Italian poets like Ariosto), in Marlowe it sparked off a visual brilliance, as in the famous description of the décor of Venus' temple in *Hero and Leander*:

> There might you see the gods in various shapes
> Committing heady riots, incests, rapes:
> For know that underneath this radiant floor
> Was Danaë's statue in a brazen tower,
> Jove slyly stealing from his sister's bed
> To dally with Idalian Ganymed,
> And for his love, Europa, bellowing loud,
> And tumbling with the rainbow in a cloud;
> Blood-quaffing Mars heaving the iron net,
> Which limping Vulcan and his Cyclops set. . . .

It was not the *Metamorphoses*, however, but the *Amores* which had most influence on Elizabethan and Jacobean poets. Speaking of the baroque poets of the early seventeenth century, Ronald Knox (himself the author of a brilliant parody of the *Heroides*[1]) remarks, in an essay on Crashaw: 'It was from Ovid, surely, that they learned their love of conceits; of singling out one incongruous feature and either throwing it into violent relief by the shock tactics of an epigram or else worrying it slowly to death under a series of alternative images'. In Milton, however, it was Ovid's poetry rather than his wit that provided the inspiration. The *Metamorphoses* was, with the Bible, the book that Milton most loved to have read to him in his blindness. To the English Augustans it was Ovid's polished urbanity and his power to describe human passion that was most appealing,

[1] *Ulixes Penelopae*, reprinted in Appendix B of R. G. Austin's edition of *Aeneid* ii (Oxford 1964).

though by then, as we have seen, he was already being
criticised for lack of naturalness. With the end of the
Augustan age in English literature Ovid fell out of favour.
To the romantics, he seemed either too lacking in spon-
taneous feeling or too flippant.

Ovid's influence on the visual arts has been equally
fertile. The painters and sculptors of the Renaissance used
the *Metamorphoses* as a kind of handbook of mythological
subject-matter. Above all it was in the Baroque age that
Ovid came into his own. With their love of the picturesque,
of movement and theatricality, the artists of the European
Baroque and Rococo found in him a never-ending fund of
inspiration for paintings, sculptures, tapestries and eventually for that most Ovidian, because most mannered, of
art-forms – the opera, in which art is allowed to create a
totally unreal world of its own.

It is this creation of a world of the imagination that is
perhaps Ovid's most lasting achievement in the *Metamorphoses*. It is a world that has its own space and time and
accepted limits. When the boy Phaethon, for instance,
wants to visit his father the Sun god, it does not take him
long to reach the land of the sunrise (i. 778–9), and the
gods fly with ease from one end of this world to the other.
As they do so it is likely that they will see some famous
mythological or historical event taking place (such as the
building of Troy, xi. 199), and no human will be surprised
to see them. Ovid gives the world of Greek and Roman
myth a new unity of landscape and atmosphere. This
explains why Gilbert Murray, in his essay 'Poiesis and
Mimesis' (*Essays and Addresses*, 1921, pp. 107–24) singles out
Ovid as supreme among the poets of pure *mimesis*, 'among all
the poets who take rank merely as story-tellers and creators
of mimic worlds'. To explain this 'merely', Professor
Murray continues: 'his criticism of life is very slight; it is
the criticism passed by a child, playing alone and peopling
the summer evening with delightful shapes, upon the

stupid nurse who drags it off to bed'. This verdict needs to be qualified. The setting of the *Metamorphoses* is indeed a world of pure imagination, but, as we have seen, the gods and nymphs and humans who move through its carefully contrived landscape are Ovid's contemporaries. Mercury, carefully combing his hair and arranging his tunic in mid-air before landing to seek Herse's favours (ii. 730–6); Perseus, outlining his social advantages to his prospective parents-in-law; Midas, the Philistine, who cannot conceive of the good life other than in terms of gold – all these must have had their counterparts in the Roman *beau monde*. Ovid passes no harsh moral judgment on them, does not vent his indignation, but his criticism of life is none the less effective for being gentle and free from explicit moralising.

P. OVIDI NASONIS

METAMORPHOSEON

LIBER UNDECIMUS

Carmine dum tali silvas animosque ferarum
Threicius vates et saxa sequentia ducit,
ecce nurus Ciconum, tectae lymphata ferinis
pectora velleribus, tumuli de vertice cernunt
Orphea percussis sociantem carmina nervis.   5
e quibus una, leves iactato crine per auras,
'en', ait 'en, hic est nostri contemptor!' et hastam
vatis Apollinei vocalia misit in ora,
quae foliis praesuta notam sine vulnere fecit;
alterius telum lapis est, qui missus in ipso   10
aere concentu victus vocisque lyraeque est
ac veluti supplex pro tam furialibus ausis
ante pedes iacuit.   sed enim temeraria crescunt
bella modusque abiit, insanaque regnat Erinys.
cunctaque tela forent cantu mollita, sed ingens   15
clamor et infracto Berecyntia tibia cornu
tympanaque et plausus et Bacchei ululatus
obstrepuere sono citharae: tum denique saxa
non exauditi rubuerunt sanguine vatis.
Ac primum attonitas etiamnum voce canentis   20
innumeras volucres anguesque agmenque ferarum
Maenades Orphei titulum rapuere triumphi.
inde cruentatis vertuntur in Orphea dextris
et coeunt ut aves, si quando luce vagantem
noctis avem cernunt, structoque utrimque theatro   25
ceu matutina cervus periturus harena
praeda canum est, vatemque petunt et fronde virentes

coniciunt thyrsos non haec in munera factos.
hae glaebas, illae direptos arbore ramos,
pars torquent silices; neu desint tela furori,   30
forte boves presso subigebant vomere terram,
nec procul hinc multo fructum sudore parantes
dura lacertosi fodiebant arva coloni.
agmine qui viso fugiunt operisque relinquunt
arma sui, vacuosque iacent dispersa per agros,   35
sarculaque rastrique graves longique ligones.
    Quae postquam rapuere ferae cornuque minaci
divulsere boves, ad vatis fata recurrunt
tendentemque manus et in illo tempore primum
inrita dicentem nec quicquam voce moventem   40
sacrilegae perimunt, perque os, pro Iuppiter! illud
auditum saxis intellectumque ferarum
sensibus in ventos anima exhalata recessit.
    Te maestae volucres, Orpheu, te turba ferarum,
te rigidi silices, te carmina saepe secutae   45
fleverunt silvae; positis te frondibus arbor
tonsa comas luxit. lacrimis quoque flumina dicunt
increvisse suis, obstrusaque carbasa pullo
naides et dryades passosque habuere capillos.
membra iacent diversa locis, caput, Hebre, lyramque   50
excipis, et (mirum!) medio dum labitur amne,
flebile nescio quid queritur lyra, flebile lingua
murmurat exanimis, respondent flebile ripae.   ⸗
    Iamque mare invectae flumen populare relinquunt
et Methymnaeae potiuntur litore Lesbi: 55
hic ferus expositum peregrinis anguis harenis
os petit et sparsos stillanti rore capillos.
tandem Phoebus adest morsusque inferre parantem
arcet et in lapidem rictus serpentis apertos
congelat et patulos, ut erant, indurat hiatus.   60
    Umbra subit terras et quae loca viderat ante,
cuncta recognoscit quaerensque per arva piorum
invenit Eurydicen cupidisque amplectitur ulnis.

hic modo coniunctis spatiantur passibus ambo,
nunc praecedentem sequitur, nunc praevius anteit   65
Eurydicenque suam iam tutus respicit Orpheus.
    Non inpune tamen scelus hoc sinit esse Lyaeus,
amissoque dolens sacrorum vate suorum
protinus in silvis matres Edonidas omnes,
quae videre nefas, torta radice ligavit;   70
quippe pedum digitos, in quantum est quaeque secuta,
traxit et in solidam detrusit acumina terram.
utque suum laqueis, quos callidus abdidit auceps,
crus ubi commisit volucris sensitque teneri,
plangitur ac trepidans adstringit vincula motu: 75
sic, ut quaeque solo defixa cohaeserat harum,
exsternata fugam frustra temptabat; at illam
lenta tenet radix exsultantemque coercet,
dumque ubi sint digiti, dum pes ubi, quaerit, et unguis,
adspicit in teretis lignum succedere suras   80
et conata femur maerenti plangere dextra
robora percussit: pectus quoque robora fiunt,
robora sunt umeri, porrectaque bracchia veros
esse putes ramos, et non fallere putando.
    Nec satis hoc Baccho est: ipsos quoque deserit agros 85
cumque choro meliore sui vineta Timoli
Pactolonque petit, quamvis non aureus illo
tempore nec caris erat invidiosus harenis.
hunc adsueta cohors, satyri bacchaeque, frequentant,
at Silenus abest: titubantem annisque meroque   90
ruricolae cepere Phryges vinctumque coronis
ad regem duxere Midān, cui Thracius Orpheus
orgia tradiderat cum Cecropio Eumolpo.
quem simul agnovit socium comitemque sacrorum,
hospitis adventu festum genialiter egit   95
per bis quinque dies et iunctas ordine noctes.
et iam stellarum sublime coegerat agmen
Lucifer undecimus, Lydos cum laetus in agros
rex venit et iuveni Silenum reddit alumno.

Huic deus optandi gratum sed inutile fecit   100
muneris arbitrium, gaudens altore recepto.
ille male usurus donis ait 'effice, quidquid
corpore contigero fulvum vertatur in aurum!'
adnuit optatis nocituraque munera solvit
Liber et indoluit, quod non meliora petisset.   105
   Laetus abit gaudetque malo Berecyntius heros
pollicitique fidem tangendo singula temptat
vixque sibi credens non alta fronde virentem
ilice detraxit virgam: virga aurea facta est;
tollit humo saxum: saxum quoque palluit auro;   110
contigit et glaebam: contactu glaeba potenti
massa fit; arentis Cereris decerpsit aristas:
aurea messis erat; demptum tenet arbore pomum:
Hesperidas donasse putes; si postibus altis
admovit digitos, postes radiare videntur;   115
ille etiam liquidis palmas ubi laverat undis,
unda fluens palmis Danaen eludere possit;
vix spes ipse suas animo capit aurea fingens
omnia. gaudenti mensas posuere ministri
exstructas dapibus nec tostae frugis egentes: 120
tum vero, sive ille sua Cerealia dextra
munera contigerat, Cerealia dona rigebant,
sive dapes avido convellere dente parabat,
lamina fulva dapes admoto dente premebat;
miscuerat puris auctorem muneris undis: 125
fusile per rictus aurum fluitare videres.
   Attonitus novitate mali divesque miserque
effugere optat opes et, quae modo voverat, odit.
copia nulla famem relevat; sitis arida guttur
urit, et inviso meritus torquetur ab auro   130
ad caelumque manus et splendida bracchia tollens
'da veniam, Lenaee pater! peccavimus', inquit,
'sed miserere, precor, speciosoque eripe damno!'
mite deum numen: Bacchus peccasse fatentem
restituit factique fide data munera solvit.   135

'neve male optato maneas circumlitus auro,
vade' ait 'ad magnis vicinum Sardibus amnem
perque iugum ripae labentibus obvius undis
carpe viam, donec venias ad fluminis ortus,
spumigeroque tuum fonti, qua plurimus exit,   140
subde caput corpusque simul, simul elue crimen.'
    Rex iussae succedit aquae: vis aurea tinxit
flumen et humano de corpore cessit in amnem.
nunc quoque iam veteris percepto semine venae
arva rigent auro madidis pallentia glaebis.   145
    Ille perosus opes silvas et rura colebat
Panaque montanis habitantem semper in antris.
pingue sed ingenium mansit, nocituraque, ut ante,
rursus erant domino stultae praecordia mentis.
nam freta prospiciens late riget arduus alto   150
Tmolus in adscensu clivoque extensus utroque
Sardibus hinc, illinc parvis finitur Hypaepis.
Pan ibi dum teneris iactat sua carmina nymphis
et leve cerata modulatur harundine carmen
ausus Apollineos prae se contemnere cantus,   155
iudice sub Tmolo certamen venit ad impar.
    Monte suo senior iudex consedit et aures
liberat arboribus: quercu coma caerula tantum
cingitur, et*pendent circum cava tempora glandes.
isque deum pecoris spectans 'in iudice' dixit   160
'nulla mora est.' calamis agrestibus insonat ille
barbaricoque Midan (aderat nam forte canenti)
carmine delenit. post hunc sacer ora retorsit
Tmolus ad os Phoebi: vultum sua silva secuta est.
ille caput flavum lauro Parnaside vinctus   165
verrit humum Tyrio saturata murice palla
instructamque fidem gemmis et dentibus Indis
sustinet a laeva, tenuit manus altera plectrum:
artificis status ipse fuit. tum stamina docto
pollice sollicitat, quorum dulcedine captus   170
Pana iubet Tmolus citharae submittere cannas.

iudicium sanctique placet sententia montis
omnibus, arguitur tamen atque iniusta vocatur
unius sermone Midae; nec Delius aures
humanam stolidas patitur retinere figuram,   175
sed trahit in spatium villisque albentibus inplet
instabilisque imas facit et dat posse moveri.
cetera sunt hominis: partem damnatur in unam
induiturque aures lente gradientis aselli.
    Ille quidem celare cupit turpique pudore   180
tempora purpureis temptat velare tiaris;
sed solitus longos ferro resecare capillos
viderat hoc famulus. qui cum nec prodere visum
dedecus auderet, cupiens efferre sub auras,
nec posset reticere tamen, secedit humumque   185
effodit et, domini quales adspexerit aures,
voce refert parva terraeque inmurmurat haustae
indiciumque suae vocis tellure regesta
obruit et scrobibus tacitus discedit opertis.
creber harundinibus tremulis ibi surgere lucus   190
coepit et, ut primum pleno maturuit anno,
prodidit agricolam: leni nam motus ab austro
obruta verba refert dominique coarguit aures.
    Ultus abit Tmolo liquidumque per aera vectus
angustum citra pontum Nepheleidos Helles   195
Laomedonteis Latoius adstitit arvis.
dextera Sigei, Roetei laeva profundi
ara Panomphaeo vetus est sacrata Tonanti:
inde novae primum moliri moenia Troiae
Laomedonta videt susceptaque magna labore   200
crescere difficili nec opes exposcere parvas
cumque tridentigero tumidi genitore profundi
mortalem induitur formam Phrygiaeque tyranno
aedificat muros pactus pro moenibus aurum.
    Stabat opus: pretium rex infitiatur et addit,   205
perfidiae cumulum, falsis periuria verbis.
'non inpune feres' rector maris inquit et omnes

inclinavit aquas ad avarae litora Troiae
inque freti formam terras conplevit opesque
abstulit agricolis et fluctibus obruit agros.   210
poena neque haec satis est: regis quoque filia monstro
poscitur aequoreo; quam dura ad saxa revinctam
vindicat Alcides promissaque munera dictos
poscit equos tantique operis mercede negata
bis periura capit superatae moenia Troiae.   215
nec, pars militiae, Telamon sine honore recessit
Hesioneque data potitur. nam coniuge Peleus
clarus erat diva: nec avi magis ille superbus
nomine quam soceri, siquidem Iovis esse nepoti
contigit haud uni, coniunx dea contigit uni.   220
    Namque senex Thetidi Proteus 'dea' dixerat 'undae,
concipe: mater eris iuvenis, qui fortibus actis
acta patris vincet maiorque vocabitur illo.'
ergo, ne quicquam mundus Iove maius haberet,
quamvis haud tepidos sub pectore senserat ignes,   225
Iuppiter aequoreae Thetidis conubia fugit
in suaque Aeaciden succedere vota nepotem
iussit et amplexus in virginis ire marinae.
    Est sinus Haemoniae curvos falcatus in arcus:
bracchia procurrunt, ubi, si foret altior unda,   230
portus erat (summis inductum est aequor harenis).
litus habet solidum, quod nec vestigia servet
nec remoretur iter nec opertum pendeat alga;
myrtea silva subest bicoloribus obsita bacis
et specus in medio (natura factus an arte,   235
ambiguum, magis arte tamen), quo saepe venire
frenato delphine sedens, Theti, nuda solebas.
illic te Peleus, ut somno vincta iacebas,
occupat et, quoniam precibus temptata repugnas,
vim parat innectens ambobus colla lacertis;   240
quodnisi venisses variatis saepe figuris
ad solitas artes, auso foret ille potitus.
sed modo tu volucris (volucrem tamen ille tenebat),

nunc gravis arbor eras (haerebat in arbore Peleus).
tertia forma fuit maculosae tigridis: illa   245
territus Aeacides a corpore bracchia solvit.
isque deos pelagi vino super aequora fuso
et pecoris fibris et fumo turis adorat,
donec Carpathius medio de gurgite vates
'Aeacide', dixit, 'thalamis potiere petitis: 250
tum modo, cum rigido sopita quiescit in antro,
ignaram laqueis vincloque innecte tenaci.
nec te decipiat centum mentita figuras,
sed preme, quidquid erit, dum, quod fuit ante, reformet!'
    Dixerat haec Proteus et condidit aequore vultum   255
admisitque suos in verba novissima fluctus.
pronus erat Titan inclinatoque tenebat
Hesperium temone fretum, cum pulchra relecto
Nereis ingreditur consueta cubilia saxo.
vix bene virgineos Peleus invaserat artus: 260
illa novat formas, donec sua membra teneri
sentit et in partes diversas bracchia tendi;
tum demum ingemuit, 'neque' ait 'sine numine vincis
exhibita estque Thetis.' confessam amplectitur heros
et potitur votis ingentique inplet Achille.   265
    Felix et nato, felix et coniuge Peleus
et cui, si demas iugulati crimina Phoci,
omnia contigerant. fraterno sanguine sontem
expulsumque domo patria Trachinia tellus
accipit. hic regnum sine vi, sine caede regebat   270
Lucifero genitore satus patriumque nitorem
ore ferens Ceyx, illo qui tempore maestus
dissimilisque sui fratrem lugebat ademptum.
quo postquam Aeacides fessus curaque viaque
venit et intravit paucis comitantibus urbem,   275
quosque greges pecorum, quae secum armenta trahebat,
haud procul a muris sub opaca valle reliquit,
copia cum facta est adeundi tecta tyranni,
velamenta manu praetendens supplice, qui sit

quoque satus, memorat, tantum sua crimina celat   280
mentiturque fugae causam: petit, urbe vel agro
se iuvet. hunc contra placido Trachinius ore
· talibus adloquitur: 'mediae quoque commoda plebi
nostra patent, Peleu, nec inhospita regna tenemus.
adicis huic animo momenta potentia, clarum   285
nomen avumque Iovem. ne tempora perde precando!
quod petis, omne feres tuaque haec pro parte vocato,
qualiacumque vides! utinam meliora videres!'
et flebat: moveat tantos quae causa dolores,
Peleusque comitesque rogant. quibus ille profatur: 290
    'Forsitan hanc volucrem, rapto quae vivit et omnes
terret aves, semper pennas habuisse putetis:
vir fuit et (tanta est animi constantia!) iam tum
acer erat belloque ferox ad vimque paratus,
nomine Daedalion. illo genitore creatis,   295
qui vocat Auroram caeloque novissimus exit,
(cura mihi pax est) pacis mihi cura tenendae
coniugiique fuit, fratri fera bella placebant:
illius virtus reges gentesque subegit,
quae nunc Thisbaeas agitat mutata columbas.   300
nata erat huic Chione, quae dotatissima forma
mille procos habuit, bis septem nubilis annis.
forte revertentes Phoebus Maiaque creatus,
ille suis Delphis, hic vertice Cylleneo,
videre hanc pariter, pariter traxere calorem.   305
spem Veneris differt in tempora noctis Apollo,
non fert ille moras virgaque movente soporem
virginis os tangit: tactu iacet illa potenti
vimque dei patitur. nox caelum sparserat astris:
Phoebus anum simulat praereptaque gaudia sumit.   310
ut sua maturus conplevit tempora venter,
alipedis de stirpe dei, versuta propago,
nascitur Autolycus furtum ingeniosus ad omne,
candida de nigris et de candentibus atra
qui facere adsuerat, patriae non degener artis;   315

nascitur e Phoebo (namque est enixa gemellos)
carmine vocali clarus citharaque Philammon.
quid peperisse duos et dis placuisse duobus
et forti genitore et progenitore nitenti
esse satam prodest? an obest quoque gloria? multis 320
obfuit, huic certe! quae se praeferre Dianae
sustinuit faciemque deae culpavit; at illi
ira ferox mota est, 'factis' que 'placebimus' inquit.
nec mora, curvavit cornu nervoque sagittam
inpulit et meritam traiecit harundine linguam.   325
lingua tacet, nec vox temptataque verba sequuntur,
conantemque loqui cum sanguine vita reliquit.
quam miser amplexans ego tum patriumque dolorem
corde tuli fratrique pio solacia misi!
quae pater haud aliter quam cautes murmura ponti   330
accipit et natam delamentatur ademptam;
ut vero ardentem vidit, quater impetus illi
in medios fuit ire rogos, quater inde repulsus
concita membra fugae mandat similisque iuvenco
spicula crabronum pressa cervice gerenti,   335
qua via nulla, ruit. iam tum mihi currere visus
plus homine est, alasque pedes sumpsisse putares.
effugit ergo omnes veloxque cupidine leti
vertice Parnasi potitur. miseratus Apollo,
cum se Daedalion saxo misisset ab alto,   340
fecit avem et subitis pendentem sustulit alis
oraque adunca dedit, curvos dedit unguibus hamos,
virtutem antiquam, maiores corpore vires,
et nunc accipiter, nulli satis aequus, in omnes
saevit aves aliisque dolens fit causa dolendi.'   345
    Quae dum Lucifero genitus miracula narrat
de consorte suo, cursu festinus anhelo
advolat armenti custos Phoceus Onetor
et 'Peleu, Peleu! magnae tibi nuntius adsum
cladis' ait. quodcumque ferat, iubet edere Peleus,   350
pendet et ipse metu trepidi Trachinius oris.

Ille refert: 'Fessos ad litora curva iuvencos
appuleram, medio cum Sol altissimus orbe
tantum respiceret, quantum superesse videret,
parsque boum fulvis genua inclinarat harenis   355
latarumque iacens campos spectabat aquarum,
pars gradibus tardis illuc errabat et illuc,
nant alii celsoque exstant super aequora collo.
templa mari subsunt nec marmore clara neque auro,
sed trabibus densis lucoque umbrosa vetusto: 360
Nereides Nereusque tenent (hos navita ponti
edidit esse deos, dum retia litore siccat).
iuncta palus huic est, densis obsessa salictis,
quam restagnantis fecit maris unda paludem.
inde fragore gravi strepitus loca proxima terret: 365
belua vasta, lupus! †iuncisque palustribus exit
oblitus et spumis et sparsus sanguine rictus,
fulmineus, rubra suffusus lumina flamma.
qui quamquam saevit pariter rabieque fameque,
acrior est rabie: neque enim ieiunia curat   370
caede boum diramque famem finire, sed omne
vulnerat armentum sternitque hostiliter omne.
pars quoque de nobis funesto saucia morsu,
dum defensamus, leto est data. sanguine litus
undaque prima rubet demugitaeque paludes. –   375
sed mora damnosa est, nec res dubitare remittit:
dum superest aliquid, cuncti coeamus et arma,
arma capessamus coniunctaque tela feramus!'
    Dixerat agrestis; nec Pelea damna movebant,
sed memor admissi Nereida conligit orbam   380
damna sua inferias exstincto mittere Phoco.
induere arma viros violentaque sumere tela
rex iubet Oetaeus; cum quis simul ipse parabat
ire, sed Alcyone coniunx excita tumultu
prosilit et nondum totos ornata capillos   385
disicit hos ipsos colloque infusa mariti,
mittat ut auxilium sine se, verbisque precatur

et lacrimis, animasque duas ut servet in una.
    Aeacides illi: 'pulchros, regina, piosque
pone metus! plena est promissi gratia vestri.   390
non placet arma mihi contra nova monstra moveri:
numen adorandum pelagi est!' erat ardua turris,
arce focus summa, fessis loca grata carinis:
adscendunt illuc stratosque in litore tauros
cum gemitu adspiciunt vastatoremque cruento   395
ore ferum, longos infectum sanguine villos.
    Inde manus tendens in aperti litora ponti
caeruleam Peleus Psamathen, ut finiat iram,
orat, opemque ferat; nec vocibus illa rogantis
flectitur Aeacidae: Thetis hanc pro coniuge supplex 400
accepit veniam; sed enim revocatus ab acri
caede lupus perstat, dulcedine sanguinis asper,
donec inhaerentem lacerae cervice iuvencae
marmore mutavit. corpus praeterque colorem
omnia servavit: lapidis color indicat illum   405
iam non esse lupum, iam non debere timeri.
nec tamen hac profugum consistere Pelea terra
fata sinunt: Magnetas adit vagus exul et illic
sumit ab Haemonio purgamina caedis Acasto.
    Interea fratrisque sui fratremque secutis   410
anxia prodigiis turbatus pectora Ceyx,
consulat ut sacras, hominum oblectamina, sortes,
ad Clarium parat ire deum; nam templa profanus
invia cum Phlegyis faciebat Delphica Phorbas.
consilii tamen ante sui, fidissima, certam   415
te facit, Alcyone; cui protinus intima frigus
ossa receperunt, buxoque simillimus ora
pallor obit, lacrimisque genae maduere profusis.
ter conata loqui ter fletibus ora rigavit,
singultuque pias interrumpente querellas   420
'quae mea culpa tuam', dixit 'carissime, mentem
vertit? ubi est, quae cura mei prior esse solebat?
iam potes Alcyone securus abesse relicta?

iam via longa placet? iam sum tibi carior absens?
at, puto, per terras iter est, tantumque dolebo,   425
non etiam metuam, curaeque timore carebunt!
aequora me terrent et ponti tristis imago:
et laceras nuper tabulas in litore vidi
et saepe in tumulis sine corpore nomina legi.
neve tuum fallax animum fiducia tangat,   430
quod socer Hippotades tibi sit, qui carcere fortes
contineat ventos et, cum velit, aequora placet!
cum semel emissi tenuerunt aequora venti,
nil illis vetitum est, incommendataque tellus
omnis et omne fretum est. caeli quoque nubila vexant   435
excutiuntque feri rutilos concursibus ignes.
quo magis hos novi (nam novi et saepe paterna
parva domo vidi), magis hos reor esse timendos.
quod tua si flecti precibus sententia nullis,
care, potest, coniunx, nimiumque es certus eundi,   440
me quoque tolle simul! certe iactabimur una,
nec nisi quae patiar, metuam, pariterque feremus,
quidquid erit, pariter super aequora lata feremur.'
　Talibus Aeolidis dictis lacrimisque movetur
sidereus coniunx; neque enim minor ignis in ipso est.   445
sed neque propositos pelagi dimittere cursus,
nec vult Alcyonen in partem adhibere pericli,
multaque respondit timidum solantia pectus.
non tamen idcirco causam probat; addidit illi
hoc quoque lenimen, quo solo flexit amantem: 450
'longa quidem est nobis omnis mora: sed tibi iuro
per patrios ignes (si me modo fata remittant!),
ante reversurum, quam luna bis inpleat orbem.'
　His ubi promissis spes est admota recursus,
protinus eductam navalibus aequore tingi   455
aptarique suis pinum iubet armamentis.
qua rursus visa, veluti praesaga futuri,
horruit Alcyone lacrimasque emisit obortas
amplexusque dedit tristique miserrima tandem

ore 'vale' dixit conlapsaque corpore toto est.   460
   Ast iuvenes, quaerente moras Ceyce, reducunt
ordinibus geminis ad fortia pectora remos
aequalique ictu scindunt freta. sustulit illa
umentes oculos stantemque in puppe relicta
concussaque manu dantem sibi signa maritum   465
prima videt redditque notas; ubi terra recessit
longius, atque oculi nequeunt cognoscere vultus,
dum licet, insequitur fugientem lumine pinum.
haec quoque ut haud poterat spatio submota videri,
vela tamen spectat summo fluitantia malo;   470
ut nec vela videt, vacuum petit anxia lectum
seque toro ponit: renovat lectusque locusque
Alcyone lacrimas et quae pars admonet absit.
   Portibus exierant, et moverat aura rudentes:
obvertit lateri pendentes navita remos   475
cornuaque in summa locat arbore totaque malo
carbasa deducit venientesque accipit auras.
   Aut minus, aut certe medium non amplius aequor
puppe secabatur, longeque erat utraque tellus,
cum mare sub noctem tumidis albescere coepit   480
fluctibus et praeceps spirare valentius Eurus.
'ardua iamdudum demittite cornua' rector
clamat 'et antemnis totum subnectite velum.'
hic iubet: inpediunt adversae iussa procellae,
nec sinit audiri vocem fragor aequoris ullam.   485
sponte tamen properant alii subducere remos,
pars munire latus, pars ventis vela negare.
egerit hic fluctus aequorque refundit in aequor,
hic rapit antemnas. quae dum sine lege geruntur,
aspera crescit hiems, omnique e parte feroces   490
bella gerunt venti fretaque indignantia miscent.
ipse pavet nec se, qui sit status, ipse fatetur
scire ratis rector, nec, quid iubeatve velitve:
tanta mali moles tantoque potentior arte est.
quippe sonant clamore viri, stridore rudentes,   495

undarum incursu gravis unda, tonitribus aether.
fluctibus erigitur caelumque aequare videtur
pontus et inductas adspergine tangere nubes;
et modo, cum fulvas ex imo vertit harenas,
concolor est illis, Stygia modo nigrior unda,   500
sternitur interdum spumisque sonantibus albet.
    Ipsa quoque his agitur vicibus Trachinia puppis,
et nunc sublimis veluti de vertice montis
despicere in valles imumque Acheronta videtur,
nunc, ubi demissam curvum circumstetit aequor,   505
suspicere inferno summum de gurgite caelum.
saepe dat ingentem fluctu latus icta fragorem
nec levius pulsata sonat, quam ferreus olim
cum laceras aries ballistave concutit arces,
utque solent sumptis incursu viribus ire   510
pectore in arma feri protentaque tela leones,
sic ubi se ventis admiserat unda coortis,
ibat in arma ratis multoque erat altior illis.
    Iamque labant cunei, spoliataque tegmine cerae
rima patet praebetque viam letalibus undis.   515
ecce cadunt largi resolutis nubibus imbres,
inque fretum credas totum descendere caelum,
inque plagas caeli tumefactum adscendere pontum.
vela madent nimbis, et cum caelestibus undis
aequoreae miscentur aquae; caret ignibus aether,   520
caecaque nox premitur tenebris hiemisque suisque.
discutiunt tamen has praebentque micantia lumen
fulmina: fulmineis ardescunt ignibus ignes.
    Dat quoque iam saltus intra cava texta carinae
fluctus; et ut miles, numero praestantior omni,   525
cum saepe adsiluit defensae moenibus urbis,
spe potitur tandem laudisque accensus amore
inter mille viros murum tamen occupat unus,
sic, ubi pulsarunt noviens latera ardua fluctus,
vastius insurgens decimae ruit impetus undae;   530
nec prius absistit fessam oppugnare carinam,

quam velut in captae descendat moenia navis.
pars igitur temptabat adhuc invadere pinum,
pars maris intus erat. trepidant haud setius omnes,
quam solet urbs aliis murum fodientibus extra   535
atque aliis murum trepidare tenentibus intus.
    Deficit ars animique cadunt, totidemque videntur,
quot veniunt fluctus, ruere atque inrumpere mortes.
non tenet hic lacrimas, stupet hic, vocat ille beatos,
funera quos maneant: hic votis numen adorat   540
bracchiaque ad caelum, quod non videt, inrita tollens
poscit opem, subeunt illi fraterque parensque,
huic cum pignoribus domus et quodcumque relictum est.
Alcyone Ceyca movet, Ceycis in ore
nulla nisi Alcyone est; et cum desideret unam,   545
gaudet abesse tamen. patriae quoque vellet ad oras
respicere inque domum supremos vertere vultus,
verum ubi sit, nescit; tanta vertigine pontus
fervet, et inducta piceis e nubibus umbra
omne latet caelum, duplicataque noctis imago est.   550
    Frangitur incursu nimbosi turbinis arbor
frangitur et regimen, spoliisque animosa superstes
unda, velut victrix, sinuataque despicit undas,
nec levius, quam siquis Athon Pindumve revolsos
sede sua totos in apertum everterit aequor,   555
praecipitata cadit pariterque et pondere et ictu
mergit in ima ratem; cum qua pars magna virorum,
gurgite pressa gravi neque in aera reddita fato
functa suo est, alii partes et membra carinae
trunca tenent: tenet ipse manu, qua sceptra solebat,   560
fragmina navigii Ceyx socerumque patremque
invocat heu! frustra. sed plurima nantis in ore est
Alcyone coniunx: illam meminitque refertque,
illius ante oculos ut agant sua corpora fluctus,
optat, et exanimis manibus tumuletur amicis.   565
dum natat, absentem, quotiens sinit hiscere fluctus,
nominat Alcyonen ipsisque inmurmurat undis.

ecce super medios fluctus niger arcus aquarum
frangitur et rupta mersum caput obruit unda.
 Lucifer obscurus nec quem cognoscere posses   570
illa luce fuit, quoniamque excedere caelo
non licuit, densis texit sua nubibus ora.
Aeolis interea tantorum ignara malorum
dinumerat noctes, et iam, quas induat ille
festinat vestes, iam quas, ubi venerit ille,   575
ipsa gerat, reditusque sibi promittit inanes.
omnibus illa quidem superis pia tura ferebat,
ante tamen cunctos Iunonis templa colebat
proque viro, qui nullus erat, veniebat ad aras
utque foret sospes coniunx suus utque rediret,   580
optabat, nullamque sibi praeferret; at illi
hoc de tot votis poterat contingere solum!
 At dea non ultra pro functo morte rogari
sustinet, utque manus funestas arceat aris,
'Iri, meae' dixit 'fidissima nuntia vocis,   585
vise soporiferam Somni velociter aulam
exstinctique iube Ceycis imagine mittat
somnia ad Alcyonen veros narrantia casus.'
 Dixerat, induitur velamina mille colorum
Iris et arcuato caelum curvamine signans   590
tecta petit iussi sub nube latentia regis.
 Est prope Cimmerios longo spelunca recessu,
mons cavus, ignavi domus et penetralia Somni,
quo numquam radiis oriens mediusve cadensve
Phoebus adire potest; nebulae caligine mixtae   595
exhalantur humo dubiaeque crepuscula lucis.
non vigil ales ibi cristati cantibus oris
evocat Auroram, nec voce silentia rumpunt
sollicitive canes canibusve sagacior anser;
non fera, non pecudes, non moti flamine rami   600
humanaeve sonum reddunt convicia linguae:
muta quies habitat; saxo tamen exit ab imo
rivus aquae Lethes, per quem cum murmure labens

invitat somnos crepitantibus unda lapillis.
ante fores antri fecunda papavera florent   605
innumeraeque herbae, quarum de lacte soporem
Nox legit et spargit per opacas umida terras.
ianua ne verso stridores cardine reddat,
nulla domo tota est, custos in limine nullus.
at medio torus est ebeno sublimis in antro,   610
plumeus, unicolor, pullo velamine tectus,
quo cubat ipse deus membris languore solutis.
hunc circa passim varias imitantia formas
somnia vana iacent totidem, quot messis aristas,
silva gerit frondes, eiectas litus harenas.   615
    Quo simul intravit manibusque obstantia virgo
somnia dimovit, vestis fulgore reluxit
sacra domus, tardaque deus gravitate iacentes
vix oculos tollens iterumque iterumque relabens
summaque percutiens nutanti pectora mento   620
excussit tandem sibi se cubitoque levatus,
quid veniat (cognovit enim), scitatur, at illa:
'Somne, quies rerum, placidissime, Somne, deorum,
pax animi, quem cura fugit, qui corpora duris
fessa ministeriis mulces reparasque labori,   625
somnia, quae veras aequant imitantia formas,
Herculea Trachine iube sub imagine regis
Alcyonen adeant simulacraque naufraga fingant.
imperat hoc Iuno.' postquam mandata peregit,
Iris abit (neque enim ulterius tolerare soporis   630
vim poterat), labique ut somnum sensit in artus,
effugit et remeat per quos modo venerat arcus.
    At pater e populo natorum mille suorum
excitat artificem simulatoremque figurae
Morphea: non illic quisquam sollertius alter   635
exprimit incessus vultumque sonumque loquendi.
adicit et vestes et consuetissima cuique
verba; sed hic solos homines imitatur, at alter
fit fera, fit volucris, fit longo corpore serpens:

hunc Icelon superi, mortale Phobetora vulgus   640
nominat. est etiam diversae tertius artis
Phantasos: ille in humum saxumque undamque trabemque,
quaeque vacant anima, fallaciter omnia transit.
regibus hi ducibusque suos ostendere vultus
nocte solent, populos alii plebemque pererrant.   645
praeterit hos senior cunctisque e fratribus unum
Morphea, qui peragat Thaumantidos edita, Somnus
eligit et rursus molli languore solutus
deposuitque caput stratoque recondidit alto.

  Ille volat nullos strepitus facientibus alis   650
per tenebras intraque morae breve tempus in urbem
pervenit Haemoniam positisque e corpore pennis
in faciem Ceycis abit sumptaque figura
luridus, exanimi similis, sine vestibus ullis
coniugis ante torum miserae stetit: uda videtur   655
barba viri, madidisque gravis fluere unda capillis.

  Tum lecto incumbens fletu super ora profuso
haec ait: 'agnoscis Ceyca, miserrima coniunx?
an mea mutata est facies? nunc respice: nosces
inveniesque tuo pro coniuge coniugis umbram.   660
nil opis, Alcyone, nobis tua vota tulerunt:
occidimus! falso tibi me promittere noli!
nubilus Aegaeo deprendit in aequore navem
auster et ingenti iactatam flamine solvit,
oraque nostra tuum frustra clamantia nomen   665
inplerunt fluctus. non haec tibi nuntiat auctor
ambiguus, non ista vagis rumoribus audis:
ipse ego fata tibi praesens mea naufragus edo.
surge, age, da lacrimas lugubriaque indue nec me
indeploratum sub inania Tartara mitte!'   670
adicit his vocem Morpheus, quam coniugis illa
crederet esse sui: fletus quoque fundere veros
visus erat gestumque manus Ceycis habebat.

  Ingemit Alcyone lacrimans, motatque lacertos
per somnum corpusque petens amplectitur auras   675

exclamatque 'mane! quo te rapis? ibimus una!'
voce sua specieque viri turbata soporem
excutit et primo, si sit, circumspicit, illic,
qui modo visus erat; nam moti voce ministri
intulerant lumen. postquam non invenit usquam,   680
percutit ora manu laniatque a pectore vestes
pectoraque ipsa ferit, nec crines solvere curat:
scindit et altrici, quae luctus causa, roganti
'nulla est Alcyone, nulla est!' ait. 'occidit una
cum Ceyce suo! solantia tollite verba!   685
naufragus interiit! vidi agnovique manusque
ad discedentem cupiens retinere tetendi.
umbra fuit, – sed et umbra tamen manifesta virique
vera mei! non ille quidem, si quaeris, habebat
adsuetos vultus nec, quo prius, ore nitebat: 690
pallentem nudumque et adhuc umente capillo
infelix vidi! stetit hoc miserabilis ipse
ecce loco!' (et quaerit, vestigia siqua supersint)
'hoc erat, animo quod divinante timebam,
et ne me fugeres, ventos sequerere, rogabam.   695
et certe vellem, quoniam periturus abibas,
me quoque duxisses! multum fuit utile tecum
ire mihi! neque enim de vitae tempore quicquam
non simul egissem, nec mors discreta fuisset.
nunc absens perii, iactor quoque fluctibus absens,   700
et sine me me pontus habet! crudelior ipso
sit mihi mens pelago, si vitam ducere nitar
longius et tanto pugnem superesse dolori.
sed neque pugnabo nec te, miserande, relinquam
et tibi nunc saltem veniam comes, inque sepulcro   705
si non urna, tamen iunget nos littera: si non
ossibus ossa meis, at nomen nomine tangam.'
    Plura dolor prohibet, verboque intervenit omni
plangor, et attonito gemitus a corde trahuntur.
    Mane erat, egreditur tectis ad litus et illum   710
maesta locum repetit, de quo spectarat euntem,

dumque moratur ibi dumque 'hic retinacula solvit,
hoc mihi discedens dedit oscula litore' dicit,
dumque notata locis reminiscitur acta fretumque
prospicit, in liquida, spatio distante, tuetur   715
nescio quid quasi corpus aqua, primoque, quid illud
esset, erat dubium; postquam paulum appulit unda,
et, quamvis aberat, corpus tamen esse liquebat,
qui foret, ignorans, quia naufragus, omine mota est
et, tamquam ignoto lacrimam daret, 'heu! miser'
      inquit,   720
'quisquis es, et siqua est coniunx tibi!' fluctibus actum
fit propius corpus: quod quo magis illa tuetur,
hoc minus et minus est amens sua, iamque propinquae
admotum terrae, iam quod cognoscere posset,
cernit: erat coniunx. 'ille est!' exclamat et una   725
ora, comas, vestem lacerat tendensque trementes
ad Ceyca manus 'sic, o carissime coniunx,
sic ad me, miserande, redis?' ait. adiacet undis
facta manu moles, quae primas aequoris undas
frangit et incursus quae praedelassat aquarum.   730
insilit huc, mirumque fuit potuisse: volabat
percutiensque levem modo natis aera pennis
stringebat summas ales miserabilis undas,
dumque volat, maesto similem plenumque querellae
ora dedere sonum tenui crepitantia rostro.   735
   Ut vero tetigit mutum et sine sanguine corpus,
dilectos artus amplexa recentibus alis
frigida nequiquam duro dedit oscula rostro.
senserit hoc Ceyx, an vultum motibus undae
tollere sit visus, populus dubitabat: at ille   740
senserat, et, tandem superis miserantibus, ambo
alite mutantur. fatis obnoxius isdem
tunc quoque mansit amor, nec coniugiale solutum est
foedus in alitibus: coeunt fiuntque parentes,
perque dies placidos hiberno tempore septem   745
incubat Alcyone pendentibus aequore nidis.

tunc iacet unda maris: ventos custodit et arcet
Aeolus egressu praestatque nepotibus aequor.
  Hos aliquis senior iunctim freta lata volantes
spectat et ad finem servatos laudat amores;   750
proximus, aut idem, si fors tulit, 'hic quoque', dixit
'quem mare carpentem substrictaque crura gerentem
adspicis' (ostendens spatiosum in guttura mergum),
'regia progenies: sunt, si descendere ad ipsum
ordine perpetuo quaeris, sunt huius origo   755
Ilus et Assaracus raptusque Iovi Ganymedes
Laomedonque senex Priamusque novissima Troiae
tempora sortitus. frater fuit Hectoris iste:
cui nisi cessissent prima nova fata iuventa,
forsitan inferius non Hectore nomen haberet,   760
quamvis est illum proles enixa Dymantis,
Aesacon umbrosa furtim peperisse sub Ida
fertur Alexirhoe, Granico nata bicorni.
  Oderat hic urbes nitidaque remotus ab aula
secretos montes et inambitiosa colebat   765
rura nec Iliacos coetus nisi rarus adibat.
non agreste tamen nec inexpugnabile amori
pectus habens silvas captatam saepe per omnes
adspicit Hesperien patria Cebrenida ripa
iniectos umeris siccantem sole capillos.   770
visa fugit nymphe, veluti perterrita fulvum
cerva lupum longeque lacu deprensa relicto
accipitrem fluvialis anas; quam Troius heros
insequitur celeremque metu celer urget amore;
ecce latens herba coluber fugientis adunco   775
dente pedem strinxit virusque in corpore liquit;
cum vita suppressa fuga est: amplectitur amens
exanimem clamatque 'piget, piget esse secutum!
sed non hoc timui, neque erat mihi vincere tanti.
perdidimus miseram nos te duo: vulnus ab angue,   780
a me causa data est! ego sum sceleratior illo,
qui tibi morte mea mortis solacia mittam.'

Dixit et e scopulo, quem rauca subederat unda,
decidit in pontum. Tethys miserata cadentem
molliter excepit nantemque per aequora pennis   785
texit, et optatae non est data copia mortis.
indignatur amans invitum vivere cogi
obstarique animae misera de sede volenti
exire, utque novas umeris adsumpserat alas,
subvolat atque iterum corpus super aequora mittit.   790
pluma levat casus: furit Aesacos inque profundum
pronus abit letique viam sine fine retemptat.
fecit amor maciem: longa internodia crurum,
longa manet cervix, caput est a corpore longe;
aequora amat, nomenque manet, quia mergitur, illi.’   795

COMMENTARY

1–84: THE DEATH OF ORPHEUS. In the tenth book Ovid described how Orpheus, bereaved of his wife Eurydice, went down to the underworld to plead with Pluto and Proserpina for her return. His singing had such charm that he was allowed to take Eurydice back, provided that he did not look at her until they emerged into the upper air. They were just about to reach the top when Orpheus glanced back, and at that moment Eurydice was lost for ever. Orpheus, inconsolable, went apart into the lonely mountains of Thrace, where, avoiding the company of women, he led rocks, animals and trees after him by the power of his song. Orpheus' songs, which make up the greater part of the tenth book (ll. 148–739) mainly tell of unnatural love, though two of the better-known stories (Pygmalion; Atalanta and Hippomenes) are only marginally connected with this theme. Book xi takes up the narrative left off at x. 147.

Summary: The Thracian Bacchantes, infuriated with Orpheus because of the contempt he has shown them, attack him and tear his body to pieces. His head and his lyre are carried down the river Hebrus and out to sea where they are washed up on the shore of Lesbos. A serpent is about to attack the head when it is turned to stone at the intervention of Apollo. The Thracian women are punished by Bacchus, who turns them into trees.

Sources and Treatment: Here, as in x. 1–85, Ovid is drawing upon versions of the Orpheus story by the Alexandrian poets Phanocles and Bion. His readers would also be familiar with Vergil's narrative in *Georgics* iv. 453–527. Ovid expands at some length and with characteristic visual detail and pointed antithesis the circumstances of Orpheus' death which Vergil relates in seven lines (ibid. 520–7). Where Vergil is content with a vague impression, Ovid is explicit. For a comparison of the two versions, see the article by C. M. Bowra in *Classical Quarterly* 1952, pp. 113ff. Bowra finds traces in Euripides and Plato of an earlier version of the story in which Orpheus is successful in recovering his wife from the underworld. Vergil and Ovid probably derive their 'tragic' version from a Hellenistic source – pathetic sentiment being more congenial to Hellenistic and Roman literary taste. Even Ovid, however, finally contrives a happy ending of a sort (see note on l. 66).

Notes:

1. *Carmine . . . tali:* the stories of unnatural love sung by Orpheus, *Met.* x. 148–739.

3. *Ciconum:* the word (a synonym for Thracians) is taken from Vergil: 'spretae Ciconum . . . matres' (*Georgics* iv. 520).

Lymphata: 'maddened'. The word is probably the Latin rendering of the Greek νυμφόληπτος, 'possessed by the nymphs'. The nymphs were supposed to inspire madness, just as the god Pan was supposed to inspire terror (cf. English 'panic'). 'Nympha' and 'lympha' were probably confused in popular etymology, which explains the odd Latin rendering.

4. *pectora:* a 'retained' accusative governed by the participle 'tectae', which is used as if it were active in meaning. Translate: 'their maddened breasts covered . . .'.

5. *sociantem:* cf. Milton, *L'Allegro:* 'Soft Lydian airs, *married* to immortal verse'.

6. *iactato crine:* the Bacchant is seen in an isolated pose as she was depicted in ancient art, with wind-tossed hair, animal skin ('ferina vellera' ll. 3–4) and the ritual thyrsus or wand ('hasta' l. 7).

7. *contemptor:* cf. *Met.* x. 79–80: 'omnemque refugerat Orpheus femineam Venerem'.

8. *Apollinei:* an adjective used, as often in verse, instead of the possessive genitive of a noun. Apollo, the god of music and art, was Orpheus' patron.

10–13. A nice conceit: the stone shows more sensitivity to music than the deranged and unfeeling Bacchants.

12. *supplex pro . . . :* 'a suppliant (asking pardon) for . . .'.

13. *sed enim:* 'none the less'.

14. *Erinys:* 'maniac fury'. The personified Erinyes or Furies, whom the Greeks euphemistically named the Eumenides or 'kindly ones', were the grim goddesses who avenged crime and took pleasure in bloodshed and war.

16. *infracto Berecyntia tibia cornu:* the use of the pipe in the worship of Bacchus was derived from the cult of the goddess Cybele, whose principal shrine was on Mt. Berecyntus in Phrygia. The Phrygian pipe was rounded off with a curving end. Cf. *Met.* iii. 533: 'adunco tibia cornu', and *Fasti* iv. 181: 'inflexo Berecyntia tibia cornu'. For the use of *infractus* (=curved) cf. Cicero *Academicae Quaestiones* ii. 79: 'infracto remo . . . commoveri'.

17. *Bacchei ululatus:* the strangeness of the metre (hiatus, and ending with a word of four syllables) is meant, perhaps, to evoke the unlovely noise of the Bacchants. Ovid is fond of such 'sound-painting'.

20. *etiamnum:* goes closely with 'canentis (Orphei)'.

21. *innumeras volucres:* cf. *Met.* x. 143, when Orpheus began to sing: 'inque ferarum / concilio medius turba volucrumque sedebat'.

22. *Orphēi:* adjective.

titulum rapuere triumphi: Ehwald, following most of the MSS, reads 'titulum rapuere *theatri*'. This can give no other meaning than that the

Maenads destroyed 'the renown of Orpheus' audience', i.e. 'Orpheus' renowned audience'. 'Theatri' suggests a semi-circular audience, but this is at variance with 'agmen' in l. 21, which indicates a line or procession (cf. 'saxa *sequentia* ducit', l. 2). I prefer Merkel's emendation 'triumphi' and translate: 'The Maenads seized on ... the line of wild beasts – the glory of Orpheus' triumph', or possibly 'Orpheus' claim to a [metaphorical] triumph.' 'Triumphi' extends the metaphor already suggested by 'agmen': the animals which follow Orpheus are seen as the triumphal procession of a victorious general. The metaphor is all the more fitting in so far as captive animals were paraded in such processions. The reading 'theatri' may have been caused by a visual confusion with 'theatro' at the end of line 25.

23. *cruentatis:* their hands are stained with the blood of the animals they have torn to pieces. Such dismemberment was part of the orgiastic rite of the Bacchants. Cf. Euripides, *Bacchae* 739.

25. *noctis avem* = 'noctuam'.

structoque: begins a new simile. Take 'ceu' first. The convention of double (or even triple) similes can be traced back to Homer. Here, a conventional nature simile is juxtaposed with one taken from contemporary Roman life. For a particularly striking juxtaposition, cf. Catullus 68, 119–28, where Laodamia's love for Protesilaus is illustrated by similes taken successively from the Roman legal system and from bird life.

structo utrimque theatro: is a circumlocution for *amphitheatro*.

26. *matutina:* the Roman shows which ended with gladiatorial contests began in the morning with the hunting (*venatio*) of wild animals. With one adjective Ovid gives his image a characteristic precision.

28. *non haec in munera factos:* not made for this service, i.e. made for a very different service.

29. 'Sum cast mee clods, sum boughs of trees, and sum threw stones'. So Golding, using his favourite ethic dative.

31. *presso:* 'down-driven'.

subigebant ... fodiebant: the imperfect tenses, suggesting quiet and steady industry, contrast with the more hectic historic present tenses which precede and follow.

33. *lacertosi:* 'brawny', 'muscular'. The adjective points the incongruity between the physical strength of the men and their terrified flight from the frenzied women.

36. Note the difference in quantity between '-quē' in the second, and '-quĕ' in the third foot. The variation is modelled on the similar use of τε in Homer.

37. *cornu ... minaci:* goes closely with 'boves' (ablative of description). Some codd. read 'cornuque minaces', which would make 'cornu' an accusative of respect: 'and tore apart the oxen that threatened them with their horns'. This gives a tighter connection to the clause (the ablative of description is awkwardly placed, in advance of the subject described). Nevertheless, with Ehwald, I retain the reading of MF.

38. *fata:* almost = 'murder'. For a similar use, cf. *Amores* i. 6, 14: 'non timeo strictas in mea fata manus'.

40. *moventem:* a nice conceit. Orpheus no longer has power to move either emotionally or (cf. ll. 1–2) physically.

41. *pro Iuppiter:* translated by Golding, never afraid of anachronism, as 'oh Lord!'

sacrilegae: the sacrilege consists in the murder of one who is the priest of Apollo and also of Bacchus (cf. l. 68).

45. Ehwald reads 'tua carmina'. On grounds of pattern and sense I prefer Bentley's emendation 'te', which, like its three preceding fellow-pronouns, is the object of 'fleverunt'. It is easy to see how 'te', in such close conjunction with 'carmina', was miscopied as 'tua'.

The repeated pronoun is characteristic of laments for the dead. Cf. *Aeneid* vii. 759–60, where the poet apostrophises the dead snake-charmer Umbro: '*te* nemus Angitiae, vitrea *te* Fucinus unda, / *te* liquidi flevere lacus'.

47. *tonsa comas:* the shaving of the hair was a sign of mourning in antiquity. This attribution of human emotion to nature was a common-place in the Hellenistic poetry which was Ovid's model. (Cf. Theocritus i. 71–2, where the jackals, wolves and lions lament for the dying Daphnis). In Vergil's version of our story (*Georgics* iv. 460–3), it is for Eurydice, not Orpheus, that physical nature laments. The two poets are using the same (Hellenistic) source, but for different purposes.

lacrimis quoque flumina dicunt increvisse suis: 'quoque' belongs to 'flumina'. For the exaggeration, cf. *Met.* i. 584, where the river-god Inachus, bewailing the disappearance of his daughter Io, 'swells his waters with his tears'. Note how with the guarded 'dicunt' Ovid amusingly antici-pates scepticism. Many Ovidian hyperboles are insured in this way against disbelief. Cf. *Met.* iii. 399 (of Echo): 'ossa *ferunt* lapidis traxisse figuram'.

48. *obstrusaque carbasa pullo:* linen robes edged with black (as a sign of mourning). This use of 'obstrusa' is rare and striking.

50. *diversa locis:* apart in place, i.e. in different places.

Hebre: apostrophe (direct address) of this kind is a favourite device of Ovid, who uses it sometimes for metrical convenience, sometimes in the interests of *variatio*.

51. *mirum!:* like 'dicunt' in l. 47, this parenthesis, in which the poet professes amazement at his own story, disarms the sceptic. Ovid often uses the parenthesis as a means of appealing to the reader, as it were, over the head of the action.

51–53. In his description of the same scene (*Georgics* iv. 523ff.) Vergil emphasises Orpheus' all-pervading concern for Eurydice: 'Eurydicen vox ipsa et frigida lingua / a! miseram Eurydicen anima fugiente vocabat, / Eurydicen toto referebant flumine ripae'. Ovid's readers were, of course, quite familiar with the Vergilian account and so could appreciate his amusingly off-hand reference ('nescio quid' has the suggestion of 'something or other') to the Vergilian Orpheus' cry of 'Eurydice!'. There is an element of subtle parody here. It is, of course, true that after stressing Orpheus' misogyny Ovid could not decently make him call upon his wife (who in any case has not been mentioned since the beginning of Book x) and so the vagueness of the 'nescio quid' is justified. To Vergil's echo effect Ovid, by a careful choice of vocabulary (*flebile . . . queritur . . . murmurat . . . exanimis*) adds a plaintive, disembodied note.

54ff. For many of the closing details of the story, Ovid is drawing on the Alexandrian poet Phanocles (*flor.* c. 330 B.C.), whose Ἔρωτες ἢ Καλοί was a collection of elegiac poems with a common theme of homosexual love. According to Phanocles, it was Orpheus' homosexuality which aroused the anger of the Thracian women (cf. *Met.* x. 83–5), who killed him and threw his head and lyre, fastened together by a nail, into the Hebrus. The lyre was washed up on the shores of Lesbos, where its sound filled the island and continued to come from the tomb where the head was buried. Ever since, explains Phanocles in aetiological vein, the island of Lesbos has been famous for its poetry and song:

> Ἐκ κείνου μολπαί τε καὶ ἱμερτὴ κιθαριστὸς
> νῆσον ἔχει, πασέων ἐστὶν ἀοιδοτάτη.
> (J. U. Powell, *Collectanea Alexandrina*, pp. 106–7).

The satirist Lucian (c. A.D. 120–180) has a story that Orpheus' lyre hung for a long time in a temple at Lesbos, where it was considered a sacrilege to lay hands on it. One day the son of the reigning tyrant tried to play it and was torn to pieces by dogs, attracted by its sound. ('Ignorant Book Collector' §§11–12).

58. *tandem*: Apollo's intervention on behalf of his protegé is certainly overdue.

62. *arva piorum*: the Elysian fields, which Roman poets after Vergil (*Aeneid* vi. 640f.) represented as part of the underworld.

64. *spatiantur*: almost 'stroll'. This pleasantly intimate note is exaggerated by Golding in his rendering of *coniunctis passibus* as 'cheek by cheek'.

65. Note how the word pattern corresponds to the sense, as Eurydice first precedes, then follows Orpheus.

66. *respicit*: the two previous lines have been leading up to this highly contrived ending. Ovid manoeuvres Orpheus into a position from which he can look back at his wife, not now with fatal results (cf. x. 57), but in the tame context of an afternoon stroll in the underworld. The happy ending is rounded off with an all too neat curtain line.

67. *Lyaeus:* one of the several cult names of Bacchus, it is a Greek word meaning 'releaser'.

68. *sacrorum vate suorum:* 'the Chapleine of his Orgies' (Golding).

71–2. A difficult passage. Either the text is corrupt or this is one of those unfinished passages which Ovid tells us he would have repolished if given the opportunity. Cf. *Tristia* i. 7.39–40: 'quicquid in his igitur vitii rude carmen habebit, / emendaturus, si licuisset, eram'.

If we take the text as it stands, Ovid seems characteristically to be visualising each Bacchante in isolation ('quaeque', 71; 'quaeque', 76): each is 'frozen' and rooted to the ground by her toes *at the point which* she reached in her pursuit ('in quantum est quaeque secuta'). It is admittedly a strain to make 'in quantum' bear this meaning. The only other possible meaning of the text as it stands is that Bacchus drew down the Bacchantes' toes *as far as* (the same distance as) each had pursued Orpheus, i.e. the length of the roots was proportionate to the length of the pursuit, but this is both bizarre and pointless. No satisfactory emendations have been suggested.

72. *traxit:* 'drew down', 'lengthened'.
acumina: translate as 'extremities'.

73f. The 'rationalised' word order would be: 'utque volucris, ubi crus suum laqueis, quos callidus auceps abdidit, commisit, sensitque teneri . . .'.

73–5. *motu:* 'with its fluttering'. Golding: 'And as the bird that finds her leg besnarled in the net. / The which the fowlers suttlelye hathe closely for her set, / And feeles shee cannot get away, stands flickering with her wings, / And with her fearfull leaping up draws closer still the strings . . .'.

78. *exsultantemque:* sound corresponds to sense. The four spondees and four double consonants give an effect of strained effort.

83. *porrectaque bracchia:* Magnus reads 'longos quoque bracchia', following M, N. The sequence 'longos . . . veros . . . ramos' is rhythmically ugly, and 'longos' is otiose. I prefer the more pointed 'porrectaque bracchia', which is the reading of F, followed by Heinsius. Translate: 'You would think her outstretched arms were real branches, and in that you would not be mistaken'.

84. *et non fallere putando:* the world of the *Metamorphoses* is where illusion turns out to be reality.
fallere: 2nd person of the future passive.

85–145: MIDAS AND THE GOLDEN TOUCH.
Summary: Bacchus abandons Thrace, the scene of Orpheus' murder, and leads his train to Lydia. His old foster-father and attendant Silenus is lost, but then returned safely to him by Midas, the king of Phrygia.

Midas, allowed to choose his own reward, asks that everything he touches may be turned to gold. When he sees its disastrous results, Midas begs for the gift to be revoked, and Bacchus assents, telling him to wash himself clean in the river Pactolus.

There is no extant version of this story earlier than Ovid, though Ovid may have drawn on an Alexandrian source. The wealth of Midas was proverbial in antiquity. His kingdom of Lydia was undoubtedly rich in gold, and under its famous king Croesus issued the first gold coinage in the Greek world – minted at Sardis, the capital. Recent excavations (1969) at Sardis have uncovered the royal mint.

Ovid's story is 'aetiological', i.e. it provides a mythical explanation (αἰτία =cause) for a well-known phenomenon (in this case, the gold deposits in the river Pactolus). In this, Ovid's model is the Alexandrian poet Callimachus, whose *Aetia* contains many stories which purport to explain the origin of obscure customs and names. For an aetiological story of our own time, cf. *How the Leopard got its Spots*, the fourth of Rudyard Kipling's *Just So Stories*.

85. *Nec satis:* not content with punishing the Bacchantes, Bacchus shakes the dust of Thrace off his feet.

86. *choro:* 'train', 'following'.

meliore: i.e. by comparison with the Bacchantes who murdered Orpheus.

sui: 'his beloved'.

89. *cohors:* a word which suggests the bodyguard (*cohors praetoria*) of a Roman general.

90. *at Silenus abest:* note how deftly Ovid uses Silenus' absence, and its explanation, to lead into the Midas story. The old satyr Silenus was Bacchus' foster-father.

91. *vinctum coronis:* perhaps a reminiscence of Vergil, *Eclogues* vi. 19. The scene, with its colourful rustic revelry, has been a favourite subject for painters. One may single out the 'Triumph of Silenus', attributed to Vandyck, in the National Gallery, London.

93. *Cecropio:* 'Athenian'. Eumolpus was the supposed founder of the Eleusinian mysteries ('orgia', l. 93), associated with Orpheus his mentor, which were celebrated at the shrine of Eleusis near Athens.

94. *simul:* = 'simulac'.

comitem . . . sacrorum: Orpheus has already been described (l. 68) as a priest of Bacchus.

95. *genialiter:* 'with good cheer'. The Romans imagined each man as having a 'genius' – a spirit similar to the guardian angel of Christian ideology. The 'genius' shared in one's pleasures and pains, hence the phrase 'genio indulgere': to enjoy oneself, treat oneself well.

97. *coegerat agmen:* 'had brought up the rear'. The departing stars are seen as an army on the march, with the morning star at the end of the column, rounding up the stragglers. For the military term, cf. Livy xxii. 2, 3: 'Hispanos et Afros ... primos ire iussit; sequi Gallos ...; novissimos ire equites; Magonem inde cogere agmen'. Cf. *Met.* ii. 114–15, where the morning star is seen as the last to leave sentry-duty ('statio') in the sky:

> diffugiunt stellae quarum agmina cogit
> Lucifer et caeli statione novissimus exit.

99. *iuveni Silenum reddit alumno:* Ovid plays on the reversal of roles, whereby the truant old foster-father (Silenus) is restored to his young ward (Bacchus).

100. *inutile:* the word means not only 'useless' but also 'doing no good' and hence positively 'harmful'. Cf. *Met.* xiii. 38 (of Palamedes, who suffered for having uncovered Ulysses' attempt to evade military service): 'sed sibi inutilior timidi commenta retexit.'

102. *usurus:* for the use of the future participle ('fated to ...') cf. 'nocitura', l. 104 infra.

104. *solvit:* 'discharged', 'paid up' (on the analogy of 'pecuniam solvere'). Curiously, in l. 135 'munera solvere' is used in the opposite sense of 'cancelling', 'revoking', a gift.

105. *Liber:* another name for Bacchus.

petisset: subjunctive because it represents the god's own thoughts ('virtual' oratio obliqua).

106. *heros:* in Latin the term, which was part of the stock epic vocabulary, means no more than 'demigod'. Midas' mother was the goddess Cybele, who was worshipped on Mt. Berecyntus in Phrygia (l. 16). Nevertheless there is an ironic undertone in the application of the language of high epic to the greedy and stupid Midas.

107. *fidem:* 'fulfilment', the faithful carrying out of a promise.

108. *non alta fronde virentem:* 'low-sprouting' ('alta fronde' is ablative of description). A characteristically precise detail: the holm-oak begins to branch out quite close to the ground.

109f. The caesura is cleverly used in these lines to suggest the pause as the king, like a child fascinated by a new toy, watches each transformation from wish to fulfilment. Note, too, the constant changes of tense and the variety and brevity of expression which suggest Midas' restless search for novelty.

112. *arentis:* accusative plural, to be taken with 'aristas'.

113. *demptum tenet:* i.e. 'demit et tenet'.

114. *Hesperidas:* the daughters of Hesperus who guarded an orchard belonging to Atlas, in the far west, in which golden apples grew. Cf. *Met.* iv. 636–7. The mythological allusion, as in l. 117, is deftly light.

117. *palmis:* ablative of separation.

Danaen: Zeus gained access to the beautiful Danaë, locked up in a tower by her father Acrisius, by taking the form of a shower of gold. The son of Zeus and Danae was Perseus.

118. *vix spes ipse suas animo capit:* Ovid's phrasing at its most deceptively simple. Midas' imagination is overwhelmed by the new prospects that open up before him.

120. *exstructas:* 'piled up'. The 'groaning board' suggests that Midas' greed was not confined to gold.

tostae frugis: bread made out of grain that was first roasted, then pounded.

124. *premebat:* 'overlaid'. The subject is 'lamina fulva'.

125. *auctorem muneris:* i.e. 'Bacchum' (='vinum'). It was a convention of epic diction to use the name of the god or goddess to denote his or her product (cf. 'Cereris', l. 112). Ovid gives this 'metonymy' a further twist by ignoring the distinction between the personification (Bacchus) and the personified (wine). The verbal wit depends on an implicit syllogism: the wine is Bacchus; Bacchus gave the gift; therefore the wine gave the gift. For other examples of the 'theological joke', where Ovid ignores the accepted distinction between the divine and human, or real and assumed, natures of a god, cf. l. 157 (Tmolus); l. 621 (Somnus).

miscuerat . . . videres: the first sentence (to 'undis'), though expressed independently, is in fact subordinate to the second ('when he mixed . . .'). Throughout this passage Ovid eschews subordination in favour of a rapid succession of short uncoordinated sentences. Cf. *Met.* xiv. 650 (Vertumnus): 'induerat scalas: lecturum poma putares.'

127. *divesque miserque:* the oxymoron sums up Midas' plight.

130. *ab auro:* 'ab' is used because the gold is not just an instrument but an independent agent.

131. *splendida:* again, the telling visual adjective. Midas' own limbs are now gold-plated (cf. l. 136, 'circumlitus auro').

132. *Lenaee:* another cult name of Bacchus (*Ληναῖος*: god of the wine-press).

133. *speciosoque . . . damno:* well rendered by Rolfe Humphries: 'save me from this loss that looks so much like gain'.

134. *mite deum numen:* note how, as often, Ovid intervenes with personal comment on his own narrative.

135. *pactique fide:* 'and as an earnest (guarantee) of what he had done'.
munera solvit: see note on l. 104 above.

136. *neve:* ='et ne'.

137. *vicinum Sardibus amnem:* the Pactolus, a river of Lydia, which flowed through the capital, Sardis.

138. *perque iugum ripae:* this reading, though disputed by Ehwald (see Appendix I), in fact makes a telling visual point, suggesting the ridged banks of a river whose stream has sunk to the bottom of its bed in summer, leaving the sand piled high on either side.

140. *plurimus:* used adverbially. 'In spate'.

141. *simul elue crimen:* spiritual purification by water was part of the rites of many religions besides Christianity, notably those of Isis, Bacchus, and Mithras. Elsewhere, referring to similar purification of various mythological heroes from blood-guilt, Ovid is sceptical about the efficacy of purely external detergents: 'a! nimium faciles, qui tristia crimina caedis / fluminea tolli posse putatis aqua!' ('How credulous to imagine that grim blood guilt can be removed by river water!'), *Fasti* ii. 45–6.

144–5. 'Even today, having absorbed the grains of the now ancient vein, the soil is caked with gold, its sods soaked yellow'.

145. *pallentia:* gold was conventionally 'pale' in Roman poetry. For the gold deposits in the river Pactolus, cf. Herodotus v. 101: 'The Pactolus is the river which brings the gold dust down from Tmolus'. Pliny (*Natural History* xxxiii. 66) mentions the Pactolus as one of five gold-bearing rivers, adding that 'there is no gold which is in a more perfect state, as it is thoroughly polished by the mere friction of the current'.

146–93: MIDAS AND THE ASS'S EARS.

Summary: Midas remains thick-witted, and in a musical contest between Pan and Apollo, ignorantly protests when Apollo is declared the winner. The god punishes him by making him grow ass's ears. Midas disguises his deformity but his barber whispers the secret into the ground and in time it is revealed.

146. *colebat:* the verb has a different meaning in relation to each of its two objects (syllepsis). With 'silvas et rura' it means 'haunt', 'frequent'; with 'Pana', 'worship'.

148. *pingue:* 'thick', 'obtuse'. Midas is the complete Philistine.

nocitura: for the use of the future participle, cf. 'usurus', l. 102.

149. *praecordia mentis:* here simply 'wits' or 'mind'.

150. *late:* goes with 'prospiciens'. Translate, 'With a wide view over the straits, Tmolus stands stiff ('riget'), steep and high to climb; stretched on either slope, it is bounded . . .'.

152. Sardis lay on the northern, and Hypaepa on the southern slopes of the Tmolus range which extended across Lydia.

153. *teneris . . . nymphis:* 'fayrye elves' (Golding).

154. *leve . . . carmen:* 'a trill or two' (Rolfe Humphries). Cf. the term 'light music'.

cerata . . . harundine: the *fistula* or pipes of Pan (Greek σύριγξ) consisted of a number of reeds of unequal length, fastened together by wax.

155. *prae se:* i.e. 'prae suis cantibus': in comparison with his own (songs)'.

156. *Tmolo:* the mountain is personified as a god. The identification is developed with playful literalness (cf. note on l. 125). The god sits on his mountain and yet at the same time he *is* the mountain: he brushes back the trees from his ears in order to hear the contestants (157–8); his hair is crowned with oak-leaves and acorns (158–9) and as he turns to look at Apollo, the forest turns with him (163–4).

certamen: for other artistic contests, cf. vi. 5–145 (Athena and Arachne: weaving), and vi. 382–400 (Apollo and Marsyas: flute-playing). Here the contest is unequal ('impar', l. 156) because Apollo, the god of song, was a lyre-player ('citharoedus'), while Pan was only a rustic piper.

157. *senior:* a variant of 'senex', used as a term of respect (cf. English 'elder'). The comparative form became general in Late Latin; hence Italian 'signor', Spanish 'señor', English 'sire', etc.

iudex consedit: 'took his seat as judge'. 'Consedit' is one of several legal terms in this passage. Cf. 'sub iudice' (l. 156), 'nulla mora est' (l. 161), 'aderat' (l. 162).

157–8. *aures liberat arboribus:* Tmolus is seen as at once man-god and mountain. Cf. the description of the river-god Achelous (viii. 549ff.), where Ovid constantly plays on different levels of personification, representing the god now as the stream itself, now as a human form inhabiting the water, now as a detached spectator unable to control it. This distinction/confusion of personification and personified can be traced back to Hellenistic poetry. For its use by Vergil, cf. *Aeneid* iv. 246–51 (Atlas, man and mountain). Such literary conceptions had their counterparts in Hellenistic and Roman art and sculpture, like the huge statue of the Nile, now in the Vatican museum, described by L. P. Wilkinson: 'The benevolent bearded god, crowned with lotus and rushes, leans on a sphinx, a cornucopia in his left hand, sheaves of corn in his right. From under his cloak the water flows out, while sixteen infants, symbolical of the sixteen cubits by which the river rises each year, disport themselves over his body...' (*The Baroque Spirit in Ancient Art and Literature*, in *Essays by Divers Hands*, vol. XXV, 1950).

158. *caerula:* Latin colour-words are notoriously elusive. Here in such close connection with 'arboribus... quercu... glandes' it must mean 'dark-green' rather than 'blue'.

159. *cava:* perhaps a reference to the fact that the temples become hollow in old age.

160–1. *in iudice... nulla mora est:* i.e. as far as the judge is concerned, there is nothing to prevent the contest beginning. For the expression, and the scene, cf. Vergil, *Eclogues* iii. 52, where Damoetas, about to begin a singing contest with Menalcas, says 'in me mora non erit ulla'.

162. *barbarico:* the word is often used in Roman poetry as a synonym for Phrygian or Trojan. The Phrygian mode of music was proverbially contrasted with the more restrained Dorian mode. The word has the secondary connotation of uncouthness; note the effective juxtaposition 'barbaricoque Midan'.

aderat: 'adesse' has the meaning of being present in court to support a friend on trial.

165–9. Ovid's word portrait, as often, is modelled on a sculptural representation: he represents Apollo with the traditional laurel wreath and long trailing robe ('palla') of the lyre player, as he appears in the statues of antiquity. The portrait may have been modelled on the statue of Apollo by Scopas set up in the temple which Augustus built on the Palatine as a thank-offering for Actium and his victory over Sextus Pompeius (cf. Propertius, ii. 31, 15; 'inter matrem deus ipse interque sororem / Pythius in longa carmina veste sonat'). The statue of Apollo Musagetes now in the Vatican Museum, if not a copy of Scopas' work, is at least of the same type.

167. Ehwald reads 'instrictamque' (after M), but such a use of 'instringere' (= to tie, bind) is unprecedented and yields little meaning. With Heinsius I prefer 'instructamque' the reading of L, N: 'a lute adorned with jewels and Indian ivory'.

169. *artificis status ipse fuit:* 'his very bearing was that of a master' (Innes).

stamina: a word that usually refers to the threads of a loom.

170. *pollice:* the lyre was usually played with the fingers, but a quill ('plectrum', l. 168) was used to obtain a louder, more resonant note.

171. *submittere cannas:* the dipping of the *fasces* ('submittere fasces') before the people, as a symbolic acknowledgement of their sovereignty, was a constitutional practice at Rome. For its supposed historical origin, cf. Livy ii. 7, 7. Ovid's phrase is a playful variation on this.

174. The punishment of Midas is depicted by Domenichino in one of the frescoes from the Villa Aldobrandini frescoes, now in the National Gallery, London. Their dream-like quality and Arcadian landscape are perfectly suited to the mood of the *Metamorphoses*.

176–7. *villisque . . . moveri:* 'And filled them full of whytish heares, and made them downe to sag, / And through too much unstablenesse continually to wag' (Golding).

posse: used as a substantive. Cf. *Met.* ii. 483, where Callisto is turned by Juno into a bear: 'posse loqui eripitur'.

179. *lente gradientis:* 'lumbering' (Innes). Note the 'pictorial' rhythm.

180. *turpique pudore:* translate, 'in shame at the disgrace'. 'Turpi' probably conceals an objective genitive. The disgrace consisted in the disfigurement or deformity.

181. *tiara:* not a 'tiara' in the English sense of the word, but an oriental cap-like headdress which was tied under the chin with broad ribbons. Golding's 'a purple nyght-cappe' is apt.

185. *nec posset reticere tamen:* 'could not keep matters to himself' – Rolfe Humphries, who adds 'no more than barbers today can do'.

190. The light rustling of the reeds is reflected in the dactylic line, with its liquid consonants and repeated 's' sounds.

192. *agricolam:* the sower or planter. Ovid effectively sustains the agricultural imagery: the barber plants his whisper in the soil, and in time the truth duly sprouts.

Epilogue: The king who grows ass's ears appears in the folk-lore of many oriental and European countries. Ovid cleverly combines this story with an account of the contest between Apollo and Pan. Midas' metamorphosis is a punishment perfectly suited to the crime: because he has no 'ear' for music Midas grows the ears of that animal which was regarded in ancient literature as pre-eminently unmusical. (Hence the Greek proverb ὄνος λυρίζων or ὄνος λύρας [ἀκούων], applied to the unmusical).

Chaucer alludes to the story in the *Wife of Bath's Tale* (952–80). Here, however, it is not Midas' barber but his wife who 'buries' the secret – the moral being that women cannot keep anything to themselves: 'Pardee, we wommen konne no thyng hele (=conceal)'.

194–220: THE FOUNDATION AND SACK OF TROY.

Summary: After punishing Midas, Apollo flies north to the Troad. Here he and Neptune help Laomedon in building the walls of Troy, but when he cheats them of their reward Neptune raises a flood and sends a sea monster to lay waste the land. To placate him, the king's daughter Hesione is exposed to the monster. After an agreement with the king, Hercules frees her but when he, too, is cheated of his reward he sacks Troy and gives Hesione in marriage to his comrade Telamon.

This short passage provides a lead into the story of Telamon's brother Peleus and the metamorphosis of Ceyx and Alcyone. Mention of Peleus also prepares the ground for the stories concerned with Achilles and Troy which are narrated in Books xii–xiv.

194. *per aera vectus:* for air travel as a means of passing from one episode to another, cf. *Met.* ii. 708ff., where Mercury flies off after turning Battus to stone: on the way, an aerial view of the beautiful Herse brings him to land. Since both the Midas and the Laomedon stories are 'timeless', non-historical myths, Ovid, wonderfully free in his use of time and space, treats them as consecutive events.

195. *citra:* on the southern (Asiatic) side, as seen from the Tmolus.

pontum Nepheleidos Helles: The Hellespont, named after Helle, the daughter of Athamas and Nephele, who was drowned there.

197. Sigeum and Rhoeteum are promontories on the Trojan coast. Here Ovid speaks, by extension, of the Sigean and Rhoetean 'deep'.

dextera and *laeva* are in opposition to 'ara'. Translate: 'on the right of Sigeum and on the left of Rhoeteum was an ancient altar . . .'.

198. *Tonanti:* The Thunderer, i.e. Jupiter, here described as Panomphaeus. The Greek term Πανομφαῖος as an epithet of Zeus probably means 'author of oracles'.

199. *novae:* the founder of Troy was Ilus, but it was his own son Laomedon who built the fortifications ('moenia'). Ovid contrives that Apollo should fly over Troy just at that moment when Laomedon is building the walls, rather as an historical novelist manoeuvres his characters on to the scene of famous events.

200. *Laomedonta:* Greek accusative.

suscepta: used as a substantive (='undertaking').

201. *nec* ='et non': the 'non' going closely with 'parvas' ('non parvas' ='magnas').

204. *aedificat:* according to *Iliad* xxi. 441ff., Jupiter sent Neptune and Apollo to spend two years in the service of men, and only Neptune built the walls, while Apollo shepherded the king's flocks. Ovid is following the version in another part of the *Iliad* (vii. 452f.) where both gods build the walls.

206. *periuria:* Laomedon denied that he had ever promised a reward.

212. *poscitur:* i.e. by Neptune and Apollo. Note how lightly and allusively Ovid treats the familiar story.

214. *equos:* horses were at once the pride and the chief export of Troy.

215. *periura:* the accusation of perfidy was commonly levelled at the Trojan people.

216. *nec:* goes with 'sine honore'.

217. *-que:* adversative 'but'.

nam: the connection of thought is: it was Telamon, not his brother Peleus, who won Hesione for his bride, because Peleus was already married. Mention of Telamon serves only to introduce his brother.

218. *avi:* Jupiter, whose son Aeacus was Peleus' father.

219. *soceri:* Nereus, whose daughter Thetis was Peleus' wife.

siquidem: 'while of course', introducing a self-evident reason.

220. *haud uni:* i.e. 'multis'.

coniunx: Peleus was the only mortal to obtain a goddess as his *formally wedded* wife.

221–65: PELEUS AND THETIS.

Summary: Proteus prophesies that Thetis will give birth to a son who will surpass his father. Jupiter is in love with Thetis but, fearing the prophecy, renounces Thetis in favour of his grandson, Peleus.

Profiting by the advice of the sea-god Proteus, Peleus defeats Thetis' attempts to escape him by her changes of shape, and wins her for his bride.

221. *Proteus:* In primitive myth Proteus represents the primordial (Πρωτεύς) water spirit. In the *Odyssey* (iv. 351) he is the old man of the sea, a kind of Davy Jones, living on the island of Pharos, a day's journey from Egypt; he tells Menelaus what will be the circumstances of his homecoming.

222. *iuvenis:* Achilles.

227. *Aeaciden:* Peleus. See note on l. 218.

229. *Est sinus:* the conventional introduction to an 'ekphrasis', or piece of narrative scene-painting. Cf. the introduction to the account of Proteus' cave in Vergil, *Georgics* iv. 387ff. (on which Ovid's version draws).

Haemoniae: Thessaly.

231. *aequor:* used to denote a calm, flat (cf. 'aequus') sea. Translate: 'the sea spreads evenly over the sand's surface'.

232–3. *servet . . . remoretur . . . pendeat:* 'generic' subjunctives.

233. *pendere:* is used here in the sense of 'hang loosely'. The sand on the sea-shore, being firm and free from damp seaweed, did not squelch or give beneath pressure.

234. *bicoloribus:* green and black.

235. *natura factus an arte:* Note the sophistication of the editorial parenthesis. Ovid describes his own description as being more like an artificial grotto than a real cave. It is 'ars' rather than 'natura' which is the back-cloth for the *Metamorphoses.* Cf. the description of Diana's grove, *Met.* iii. 158–9: 'simulaverat artem ingenio natura suo'. Ovid's art simulates nature but improves upon it in the arrangement of landscape features. The way in which Ovid, like a connoisseur of landscape gardening, measures up the relative influence of *natura* and *ars*, deciding on balance in favour of *ars*, is characteristically mannered. For another, comically incongruous example of fine distinction-making, cf. ll. 369–70 (the herdsman's description of the marauding wolf): 'quamquam saevit pariter rabieque fameque, acrior est rabie'.

237. *frenato delphine:* a 'bridled dolphin', such as those depicted in contemporary frescoes.

241–6. For Thetis' rapid changes of shape, cf. those of Proteus, *Met.* viii. 730–7, described by Achelous. The power of self-transformation attributed to sea-gods reflects perhaps the changeability and unpredictability of the sea itself.

The rapidity of Thetis' self-transformations and Peleus' matching moves is reflected in the pace of ll. 243–5, at the rate of one metamorphosis to a line. The sounds and rhythms are adapted to the images: l. 243 is suitably fluttering, and l. 244 gets off to a heavy start with a cluster of four consonants in the first foot.

249. *Carpathius vates:* Proteus.

252. Proteus is passing on the instructions by means of which he himself was caught by Aristaeus. Cf. Cyrene's instructions to Aristaeus, her son, Vergil, *Georgics* iv. 411ff.

257. *pronus:* 'sinking'.

Titan: the sun-god, here represented as driving his chariot down to the western sea at evening. Cf. *Met.* ii. 67ff.

264. *exhibita estque:* 'but Thetis is discovered!' For the adversative '-que', cf. l. 217.

266–409. PELEUS AT THE COURT OF CEYX.

The episode falls into three parts, (i) the circumstances of Peleus' arrival at the court of Ceyx (ll. 266–90); (ii) the story of Daedalion and Chione, told by Ceyx to his guest (ll. 291–345); (iii) the story of the ravening wolf sent to avenge the murder of Peleus' half-brother, and Peleus' eventual absolution from guilt (ll. 346–409).

(i) **266–90.** *Summary:* Telamon and Peleus have killed their half-brother Phocus, son of Aeacus and the nymph Psamathe, and are forced to flee their home. Peleus takes refuge at the court of Ceyx, king of Trachis, where he is hospitably received though he does not reveal the cause of his exile.

267. *crimina:* here, 'offence', 'crime'. Note that again Ovid uses the *exception* as a linking device. Peleus was happy in everything except his murder of Phocus, but it is this that brings him to Trachis.

268. *contigerant:* here, as in l. 220, used of good fortune: 'whose life had been all prosperity' (Innes).

271. *nitorem:* 'shining brightness'. When Peleus arrives, Ceyx' resplendence is uncharacteristically overcast ('dissimilisque sui', l. 273) in mourning for his brother.

274–81. In this long sentence, 'postquam' governs the three verbs 'venit', 'intravit', and 'reliquit', while the main verb is 'memorat'.

276–7. The objects of 'reliquit' are 'greges' and 'armenta', the antecedents of 'quos' . . . 'quae'.

277. *sub:* 'down in'.

279. *velamenta:* it was the custom for suppliants to carry branches of olive or laurel wound round with wool which also covered the hands.

282. *placido . . . ore:* peace (cf. l. 297, 'cura mihi *pax* est') and light (cf. l. 271) are Ceyx' essential characteristics.

283. *commoda:* 'amenities'.

mediae quoque plebi: 'ordinary folk'. Ceyx, very much the 'grand seigneur' (note his use of the royal 'we': 'nostra . . . tenemus'), is impressed by Peleus' pedigree. Ovid transposes the class distinctions of contemporary Rome to the world of myth. Thus even his Olympus has its own 'plebs' (*Met.* i. 173) or lower-class gods.

285–6. Ceyx' naturally welcoming attitude ('huic animo') is reinforced by Peleus' decisive claims ('momenta') – fame and divine origin. For the meaning of 'momentum' (= 'movimentum'), cf. Lucan, *Pharsalia* iv. 819: 'momentumque fuit mutatus Curio rerum', i.e. Curio's change of loyalty *turned the scales*, was the decisive factor, in the struggle between Caesar and the senate.

287. *haec:* demonstrative. Ceyx indicates his possessions with a wave of the hand.

vocato: an example of the so-called future imperative, rather archaic in tone.

288. *qualiacumque:* 'such as it is', deprecating.

289. *flebat:* 'began to weep'.

290. *quē . . . quĕ:* see note on l. 36.

(ii) 291–345. *Summary:* Ceyx tells how his brother Daedalion was turned into a falcon. Daedalion's daughter Chione was loved by the gods Mercury and Apollo, and gave birth to twins. In her pride, she boasted that her beauty was superior to that of Diana. When the goddess punished her with death, Daedalion threw himself off a high rock, but in his fall was turned, by Apollo, into a falcon. The story within a story is a favourite device of Ovid. The fact that this is the first of three consecutive 'ornithological' metamorphoses (the others being of Ceyx and Alcyone and of Aesacus) is more than coincidental and suggests that Ovid is here drawing on the *Ornithogonia* (stories of transformation of humans into birds) by the Hellenistic poet Boeo, or the Latin version of it by Aemilius Macer, an older contemporary of Ovid.

291. *hanc:* again demonstrative. Ceyx points to the falcon fluttering above.

293. *tanta est animi constantia:* 'so unchanging is character'. Daedalion was as fierce in his human state ('iam tum') as he is now when a falcon. This continuity of character which survives metamorphosis is a marked feature of Boeo's *Ornithogonia.* Cf. A. C. Hollis on *Met.* viii. 236.

tantum = 'tam' (as).

295–8. The structure of the sentence is complicated but reflects in the order of words a unity (the brothers' common origin) that becomes divided (by the difference of their characters and interests). The single *creatis* is in opposition to the separate *mihi* and *fratri* in the following lines.

genitore: Lucifer, the Morning-star ('qui vocat Auroram'), who is at the same time the Evening-star ('caeloque novissimus exit'). The only two surviving lines of Cicero's 'Alcyone' epyllion also refer to Ceyx as the son of the morning star:

> hunc genuit clam . . . dis delapsus ab astris
> praevius Aurorae solis noctisque satelles.

299. *illius virtus:* i.e. 'ille virtute'.

300. *Thisbaeas:* after Thisbe, a town in Boeotia which Homer (Iliad ii. 502) describes as 'dove-haunted'. As Davies remarks, Roman poets used recondite literary epithets such as this not to define or illumine the object described, but to evoke the Homeric original or to display erudition. Such epithets, as Milton shows, also lend decoration to the verse.

302. Roman girls were usually married between the ages of thirteen and sixteen or seventeen.

303. *Maia . . . creatus:* Mercury.

304. *Cylleneo:* Cyllene is a mountain in Arcadia on which Maia gave birth to Mercury.

307. *ille:* Mercury.

310. *anum simulat:* i.e. he disguises himself as an old woman.

312. *versuta propago:* translated by Golding as 'a wylye pye' (pye = magpie, thief).

313. *Autolycus:* in the *Odyssey* he appears as Odysseus' maternal grandfather, 'who excelled all men in thievery and in oaths. It was a god, Hermes, who had given him this skill'. His ability to change black into white and vice versa derives from Euripides (fr. 282–4). Shakespeare, who was certainly familiar with Golding's *Metamorphoses*, if not with Chapman's *Odyssey*, used the name for his charming rogue in *The Winter's Tale*, the pedlar Autolycus, 'littered under Mercury . . . a snapper-up of unconsidered trifles'.

furtum ingeniosus ad omne: 'up to all manner of tricks' (Innes).

316. *namque . . . gemellos:* Ovid is a master of the 'throw-away' line.

319. *nitenti:* i.e. Lucifer, her grandfather (see ll. 295–6). Ehwald reads 'progenitore Tonanti'. 'Tonans' can only refer to Jupiter, but Lucifer (cf. ll. 295–6), not Jupiter, was Chione's grandfather ('progenitor', placed here in such close connection with 'genitor', must mean grandfather and not merely ancestor). With Bentley therefore I prefer the reading 'nitenti' (= 'Lucifero').

322. *sustinuit:* 'dared to'.

culpavit: not 'blamed' but 'found fault with'.

323. *factis . . . placebimus:* i.e. 'If she doesn't like my looks, perhaps my deeds will please her better!' The savage irony is typical of Ovid's goddesses, who show no mercy to the unfortunates who dare to cross them. Note that the '-que' in 'factisque' is not part of Diana's words but connects them with what precedes – an Ovidian idiosyncrasy.

325. *meritam:* translate as 'guilty'.

328–9. *patrium:* i.e. Ceyx, who was on the spot, bore all the grief that the girl's father would have felt, had he been there. Translate: 'Then sadly putting my arms around her, I bore a father's grief in my heart and sent words of consolation to my brother, so devoted to his child'.

misi: implies that Daedalion was absent when his daughter died.

-que . . . -que = 'et . . . et'.

331. *accipit:* 'heeded'.

332. *ardentem:* sc. 'Chionen', on the funeral pyre.

332–3. *impetus illi . . . fuit:* i.e. 'conabatur'.

334. *concita membra fugae mandat:* 'he dashed off in frenzied flight' (Innes).

335. *spicula:* is the object of 'gerenti'.

pressa: ablative, with 'cervice': 'lowered', or 'bowed'.

336. *iam tum:* i.e. even before his metamorphosis. Note how natural and almost imperceptible the metamorphosis is made to seem, as described by a spectator (Ceyx). The 'putares' draws the reader, too, into the scene.

plus homine: i.e. 'plus quam pro homine'.

339. *Parnasi:* Parnassus is almost forty miles south of Trachis, the scene of the metamorphosis, but the poet is not concerned with authenticity of geographical detail.

miseratus: this emphasis on pity as the motive for divine intervention to produce metamorphosis is characteristic of Boeo's *Ornithogonia*, to judge from surviving paraphrases. Cf. A. C. Hollis on *Met.* viii. 251–9.

341. *subitis:* i.e. newly sprouted.

pendentem: 'hovering'.

343. *antiquam:* i.e. the courage he had formerly, as a man. Cf. l. 293 and note.

344. *nulli satis aequus:* literally 'sufficiently well-disposed to none', i.e. 'hostile to all [birds]'. Magnus reads 'nullis satus aequus'; i.e. the falcon, by nature, is like no other bird. It is difficult to take 'satus' as synonymous with 'natus'. Though not clear, the best MSS favour the reading given here.

345. In rhetorical style, Ovid likes to end a speech or a story with an arresting, resounding 'curtain line'. For another example of the repetition effect ('dolens . . . dolendi'), also linked with a change of roles cf. *Met.* viii. 724, where Philemon and Baucis, the guardians of a shrine, are turned into trees and themselves become the objects of veneration: 'Cura deum di sint, et qui coluere colantur'.

(iii) 346–409. *Summary:* When Ceyx has finished his story, Peleus' cowherd runs in with the news that a murderous wolf has attacked his cattle on the shore. Peleus sees in this the hand of his stepmother Psamathe, seeking vengeance for her murdered son. He prays her to soften her anger, but she does so only when Thetis intercedes. The wolf is turned to stone and Peleus leaves for Magnesia, where he is eventually absolved from blood-guilt by King Acastus.

349ff. Golding, always ready to add colour and characterisation of his own, makes the herdsman a country bumpkin who speaks broad Mummerset (see note on ll. 357–8). Such characterisation is alien to Latin poetry. Ovid's herdsman is funny not because he speaks an appropriate yokel language but precisely because he speaks an inappropriate language of high-flown, exaggerated solemnity. The situation calls for quick and decisive action, but the herdsman spends twenty-three long-winded lines in describing the scenery before declaring that there is no time to lose ('mora damnosa est', l. 376). Thus the humour consists in the very incongruity between the words and the situation. The whole speech reads like a parody of the traditional messenger-speech of tragedy.

350. Note how the 'cladis' is kept in suspense.

351. *pendet:* 'hung on his words'. Even Ceyx ('ipse Trachinius') feels for his guest, and shows a look of fear in his face ('trepidi oris': genitive of quality).

354. i.e. at noon, when the sun has as much of his course to look forward to as to look back on. The circumlocution only develops what has already been said in 'medio . . . sol altissimus orbe'. For the parody of bombastic circumlocution, cf. *Hamlet*, Act 3, Scene 2:

> Full thirty times hath Phoebus' cart gone round
> Neptune's salt wash and Tellus' orbed ground,
> And thirty dozen moons with borrow'd sheen
> About the world have times twelve thirties been.

357–8. 'Zum roayled zoftly up and downe, and zum a them did zwim, / And bare their jolly horned heades aboove the water trim' – so Golding's rustic cowherd.

359. *subsunt:* 'lies close to'.

361. *Nereides:* Psamathe, whose son Phocus had been killed by Peleus (cf. l. 267), was a Nereid or sea-nymph. It was therefore appropriate that the wolf who was to be the instrument of her revenge (l. 366) should come from the vicinity of her temple.

ponti: goes closely with 'deos': 'gods of that sea', i.e. the Malian gulf, on the Thessalian coast.

362. *edidit:* sc. 'mihi': 'told me'.

366. *iuncisque palustribus:* the MSS. are corrupt. Magnus reads 'niveisque paludibus' (following M), but it is difficult to apply the adjective 'niveus' (= 'clear', 'pellucid') to a marsh ('palus'); if it refers to the *water* of the marsh, then we have the improbability of the wolf emerging from water. Of the various conjectures, I prefer Korn's 'iuncisque palustribus': 'marsh reeds' (cf. 'iuncique palustres', *Met.* viii. 336). Translate: 'it came out of the marsh reeds smeared with foam, its jaws flecked with blood'.

367–8. *rictus . . . lumina:* accusatives of the 'part affected'.

369. *qui quamquam . . . rabie:* with absurdly incongruous pedantry, Ovid's cowherd pauses to measure the wolf's 'rabies' against its 'fames'.

370. *curat:* 'choose to', 'take the trouble to' – a rather fastidious word to use of a ravening wolf.

373. *pars quoque de nobis:* Ehwald sees in this a trace of vulgar Latin, suited to the rustic character of the herdsman. Though the use of 'de' with the ablative in place of the genitive was characteristic of vulgar Latin (from which it passed into the Romance languages) it is also used by the poets simply to suit metrical requirements. Cf. for instance *Epistulae ex Ponto* iv. 13.23: 'laudes de Caesare'. The herdsman's speech is comically effective precisely because it is so un-rustic both in style and diction.

374. *leto est data:* = 'occisa est'. The phrase has an archaic, high-sounding ring to it. Cf. Cicero, *de Legibus* ii. 9.22, where the author is deliberately using an archaic legal language.

375. *demugitae:* 'filled with bellowing'. A word invented by Ovid for the occasion, it is ludicrously ill-fitted to the passive voice.

undaque prima: 'the water's edge'.

377–8. The solemn repetition of 'arma' (cf. Vergil, *Aeneid* ii. 668), and the rare use of 'capessere' (found nowhere else in the *Met.*) is consonant with the messenger's high-flown style.

coniunctaque: a transferred epithet, which can be retained in translation: 'let us make a combined attack'.

380. *admissi:* Peleus' murder of Phocus, whose mother, the Nereid Psamathe, is now seeking vengeance.

381. *damna sua:* 'his (Peleus') losses'.

383. *rex Oetaeus:* Ceyx. Trachis was near Mt. Oeta.

384. *Alcyone:* the first appearance of the leading character of the story of ll. 410–748. Already she is characterised by a nervous and clinging devotion to her husband.

385. *prosilit:* the rapid movement which the word suggests, anticipates the circumstances of Alcyone's metamorphosis into a bird. Cf. 731: '*insilit* huc, mirumque fuit potuisse'. This continuity between the human and the animal characteristics of Alcyone gives her eventual metamorphosis its seeming inevitability.

nondum totas ornata capillos: Alcyone is described as if she were a fashionable Roman lady, with much time to devote to the arrangement of her hair.

388. *animasque duas ut servet in una:* the concept is central to the Ceyx and Alcyone story, and reaches its climax in ll. 700–1. This idea of the lives of the two lovers united in one is a favourite theme of Latin elegy, the spirit of which imbues the Ceyx and Alcyone episode. For the motif, cf. Propertius ii. 28b, 42: 'vivam si vivet; si cadet illa, cadam'; and *Heroides* xi. 60 (Canace reminding Macareus of his own words): 'vive, nec unius corpore perde duos'.

389. *Aeacides:* Peleus.

pulchros: 'becoming'. The word is often used to denote moral beauty.

390. *plena est promissi gratia vestri:* 'the favour contained in your promise is ample', i.e. it is enough that you and your husband have offered assistance already; there is no need for violent action.

391. *nova monstra:* 'this strange portent'.

392. *numen pelagi:* i.e. Psamathe, the Nereid.

393. *focus:* a lighthouse.

395–6. *vastatoremque . . . ferum:* 'the cruel stroygood' (Golding).

401. *sed enim:* 'however'.

revocatus: the participle has a concessive force: 'though recalled'.

402. *dulcedine sanguinis asper:* 'wild with the sweet taste of blood'. 'dulcedine . . . asper' is an oxymoron, for 'asper' can connote bitterness.

404. *mutavit:* the subject is Psamathe. For the wolf turned to stone, cf. Homer's story of the Phaeacian ship turned to stone (*Odyssey* xiii. 156). Davies comments: 'Stories of this kind were suggested by the resemblance, real or fancied, of a rock, stone or other natural object to the animal or object in question'.

409. *Haemonio:* = 'Thessalico'.

purgamina caedis: the blood guilty could not be admitted to the worship of the gods before they had been purified with fire, salt water, and sulphur at the hands of an innocent man. For Peleus' purification by Acastus, see *Fasti* ii. 39–40:

> ipsum quoque Pelea Phoci
> caede per Haemonias solvit Acastus aquas.

410–748. THE CEYX AND ALCYONE IDYLL.

This is one of the most perfectly shaped stories in the *Metamorphoses*. For his version of the legend Ovid seems to have drawn on Nicander, the Greek author (*floruit* c. 150 B.C.) of a work on metamorphoses called 'Ἑτεροιούμενα. Nicander had a patriotic interest in the Ceyx episode, because his native town Colophon was near Claros, a town which contained the famous temple of Apollo to which Ceyx went on pilgrimage (cf. l. 413).

The story falls into four main sections: (i) Ceyx' departure and Alcyone's sorrow (ll. 410–73); (ii) the storm, and drowning of Ceyx (ll. 474–572); (iii) the dream episode in which Alcyone learns of her husband's death (ll. 573–673); (iv) Alcyone's grief on waking, her visit to the shore and recognition of her husband's body, and the transformation of husband and wife into halcyon birds (ll. 674–748). The arrangement is not unlike that of a symphony, the slower movements (i) and (iii) alternating with two highly charged episodes, one of storm and stress, the other of climactic emotion. Not only in its theme (the exclusive devotion of lovers parted by a sea voyage) but also in its treatment, the episode owes as much to elegy as to epic. Though the usual fanciful ingenuity is not absent, the tone of the passage is remarkably consistent in its pathos. This balance is only disturbed by the perhaps over-long storm *ekphrasis*, in which Ovid seizes the opportunity for a bravura display of the epic style. There were two ancient versions of the story. According to Apollodorus, in his learned study of mythology (*Bibliotheca* vii. 4), Ceyx and Alcyone were turned into birds as a punishment for their presumption in calling each other Zeus and Hera. In the version related by Lucian (*Halcyon*, i) and Dionysius Periegetes (*de Aucupio*, ii, 8) Alcyone, lamenting for her drowned husband, is granted wings by the gods so that as a halcyon she can search the seas for him. It is this second version that reached Ovid, probably through Nicander.

(i) **410–73.** *Summary:* Ceyx, disturbed by the strange events which have troubled his land, decides to go to Claros to consult the oracle of Apollo. His wife Alcyone begs him not to make the sea voyage. Her anxieties are allayed when he promises to return within two months, but when he finally departs she is inconsolable.

410. *fratrisque sui:* 'vaguely defines *prodigiis*' (Davies): 'the strange fate of his brother' (Daedalion, turned into a hawk. Cf. ll. 291–345).

fratremque secutis: also goes with 'prodigiis': 'the strange events that followed his brother's death', i.e. the marauding wolf and its petrifaction.

413. *nam:* the thought connection is 'he did not go to the (more famous) oracle at Delphi, for. . .'. For the purposes of the story Ceyx has to make a journey by sea there to perish in a storm; Phorbas and his Phlegyan bandits are only introduced to provide this voyage with specious motivation.

416. *Alcyone:* the sudden change to direct address (apostrophe) creates a mood of solicitude for, and involvement with the heroine.

417. *buxoque simillimus ora:* a stock Ovidian simile. Cf. *Met.* iv. 134–5 where Thisbe finds the dead body of her lover Pyramus: 'oraque buxo / pallidiora gerens exhorruit'.

420. The double liquid consonants (*rr, ll*) echo the trembling sobs.

421–43. Alcyone's speech of reproach, like much else in this episode (cf. ll. 431, 441, 473) is elegiac rather than epic in inspiration. Distress at the prospect of an impending sea voyage by the loved one is a frequent motif in Latin elegy. Cf. Propertius i. 8.1, where the poet, in the same style, accuses Cynthia (about to sail for Illyria) of cruelty: 'Tune igitur demens, nec te mea cura moratur?'

423. *securus:* 'untroubled'. The primary meaning of the word is subjective, denoting a freedom from care ('se' + 'cura').

Alcyone: the use of the proper name appeals to Ceyx' finer feelings. The personal pronoun 'me' might suggest rather selfish motives on Alcyone's part.

425. *at puto:* like the 'at credo' of prose rhetoric, introduces an imaginary interjection. The sense is: 'suppose your journey was by land, I would have no reason for fear, only for grief at the parting. But as it is, you are going by sea, and I am terrified of the sea'.

429. *tumulis sine corpore:* i.e. cenotaphs (κενοτάφια) – empty tombs set up in memory of those lost at sea. The horror of death by drowning at sea is a common theme of Greek and Latin literature. Cf. Homer, *Iliad* xxi. 249; *Odyssey* v. 311; Vergil, *Aeneid* i. 96ff. Elsewhere (*Tristia* i. 2, 51ff.) Ovid gives the reason for this horror: it is not death which is to be feared, but the loss of funeral rites: 'hoc letum timeo; genus est miserabile leti'.

431. *Hippotades:* Alcyone was the daughter of Aeolus, lord of the winds, and thus grand-daughter of Hippotes. Here she tells her husband that when he is at the mercy of the sea, family influence (the fact that he is the son-in-law of the god of the winds) will not protect him from the threat of storms. In contrast with *Aeneid* i. 34ff. where the storm is motivated by the private spite of Juno, who uses her personal influence with Aeolus to have the winds let loose, Ovid from the very beginning of this story stresses the completely impersonal power of the forces of nature. Aeolus himself appears nowhere in the actual account of the storm, and the mythical machinery of conventional epic is notably absent. This makes the predicament of Ceyx and Alcyone a more vulnerable one: they are completely at the mercy of the blind elements, and can hope for no *deus ex machina*. All they have is their mutual love, frail in opposition to the powers of nature but eventually, as it turns out, victorious.

432. *placet:* like 'contineat', subjunctive by assimilation to the mood of 'sit'.

434. *incommendata:* 'defenceless'. A word found only here.

435. *vexant:* the subject is still 'venti'. For the idea that lightning is produced by the friction of clouds under pressure from wind, cf. *Met.* i. 56.

437-8. *saepe . . . vidi:* a homely touch, well rendered by Golding: 'right well I know theyr powre, / And saw them oft a little wench within my fathers bowre'.

439. *quod . . . si:* 'but if'.

441-3. The same determination of the lover to follow the loved one, to share the dangers of sea voyage, is a motif of elegy. Cf. Propertius ii. 26, 29-30: 'seu mare per longum mea cogitet ire puella, / hanc sequar et fidos una aget aura duos'. It is interesting to compare the present passage with Ovid's autobiographical account of his own wife's grief at his departure for exile, when she plays Alcyone to his Ceyx:

> 'non potes avelli, simul hinc, simul ibimus': inquit,
> 'te sequar, et coniunx exulis exul ero'.
>
> (*Tristia* i. 3, 81-2)

It is ironic that even when he is describing his own personal tragedy, Ovid should see himself in terms of one of his own poetic characters.

445. *sidereus:* Ceyx is the son of Lucifer, the morning star. Cf. ll. 452, 570.

ignis: the use of this word in close connection with 'sidereus' involves a play upon words. In the context the word refers to the fire of love, but it can also be used of a star (cf. 'per patrios ignes', l. 452).

447. *in partem adhibere pericili:* 'to involve in danger'.

448. Here and elsewhere (ll. 270, 282, 461) Ovid delicately suggests the quiet, sympathetic character of Ceyx. His love may be more sparingly expressed than his wife's, but it is as true.

449. *causam probat:* 'probare aliquid alicui' = to convince someone of the rightness of something.

456. *armamentis:* the dispondaic ending is rare in Ovid where a purely Latin word is concerned – as opposed to a Greek proper name. For frequent parallels one must go back to the earlier neoteric, experimental style of Catullus, who in his *Peleus and Thetis* has no fewer than thirty spondaic fifth feet. In these lines Ovid uses the unusual rhythm simply for the sake of variety.

457. *rursus:* goes with 'horruit'.

461. *iuvenes:* 'the crew'.

quaerente moras Ceyce: cf. note above on l. 448. To soften the blow for his wife, Ceyx seeks excuses for delay.

462. *ordinibus geminis:* 'gemini' can be simply synonymous with 'duo' (cf. *Met.* xv. 739: 'scinditur in geminas partes circumfluus amnis'), in which case the rowers may be seen as sitting in two ranks (one on either side of the ship). It is possible, however, that Ovid is referring, anachronistically, to a bireme vessel with a double bank of oars on either side.

463. Metrically, a curious line. The regular spondees and the repeated *q, c, t* sounds may be said to reproduce the regular, slicing action of the oar-blades. The end of the fourth foot also corresponds with the end of a word – a rare example of the so-called 'bucolic diaeresis' (bucolic because it occurs mainly in pastoral poetry, both Greek and Latin). Here the metrical break coincides with a cinematic 'cut' from sea to shore.

464. *relicta:* nominative, describing Alcyone.

466. *prima:* again, to be taken with the subject. 'She is the first to see . . .' Alcyone's love makes her keener-sighted than her fellow-spectators. This gives more point than to take 'prima' with 'signa': 'she sees her husband waving a first farewell'.

redditque notas: 'and returns his waves'. For 'nota' as a sign of greeting, cf. *Ars Amatoria* iii. 514, where the poet advises a girl to acknowledge her lover's nods (winks?): 'innuet; acceptas tu quoque redde notas'.

473. *quae pars admonet absit:* without her husband, Alcyone is incomplete.

This departure scene borrows several details from the passage in *Heroides* xiii where Laodamia tells Protesilaus how she saw him sail away from her. However, in comparison with the present lines, where Ceyx' departure is vividly realised and Alcyone's grief reflects her emotional absorption in Ceyx, the Laodamia episode seems contrived. The heroine is less interested in Protesilaus than in her own emotions. Note, e.g. ll. 23-4: 'Lux quoque tecum abiit, tenebrisque exsanguis obortis / succiduo *dicor* procubuisse genu'. ('When you disappeared the light disappeared with you and I *am told* I fell forward on sinking knees, pale and swooning'). Ceyx' departure is described in terms which are closer to elegy than to epic. Epic leavetakings are usually restrained, and narrated chronologically, whereas elegy describes the scene dramatically and gives the leave-takers free-er emotional rein. Here, in the Ceyx and Alcyone story, Ovid turns elegiac conventions to the service of narrative epic.

(ii) **474-572.** *Summary:* When Ceyx' ship is out at sea, a storm blows up and soon all is confusion. In spite of the crew's desperate efforts, the ship founders. Ceyx drowns, praying with his last words that the waves may carry his body to Alcyone. The storm scene was a recognised 'set-piece' within the epic tradition, and Ovid's description follows a conventional pattern. His particular model is *Aeneid* i. 84ff., though many elements may be traced back to the storm scene in Pacuvius' *Teucer*. As far as violence goes, Pacuvius leaves his successors little room for improvement:

> flamma inter nubes coruscat, caelum tonitru contremit,
> grando mixta imbri largifico subita praecipitans cadit,
> undique omnes venti erumpunt, saevi existunt turbines,
> fervit aestu pelagus.

> (Loeb *Remains of Old Latin*,
> ed. E. H. Warmington, vol. 2, p. 294)

474. *Portibus exierant:* Ovid, being primarily a visual artist, uses an almost cinematic technique, 'cutting' from Alcyone's bedchamber to the ship. The transition is smoothly effected by a skilful use of tenses: Alcyone returns to her lonely bedchamber (present tenses) while Ceyx' crew, who had by now reached the open sea (pluperfect), turn in their oars alongside and unfurl the sails (present again).

475. *obvertit lateri:* the oars are turned alongside the ship. It is only later when the storm breaks that they are taken inside the ship (l. 488) and the oarholes are stopped up (487: 'pars munire latus').

476. Translate 'sets the yard-arm ('cornua') at the mast-top, unfurls all canvas from the mast and catches the favouring breeze'.

478. *medium . . . aequor:* i.e. half the distance.

479. *utraque tellus:* i.e. their point of departure and their destination.

487. *ventis vela negare:* i.e. they reef the sails.

488-9. *hic . . . hic:* cf. the similar technique in *Aeneid* i. 106-7: '*hi* summo in fluctu pendent; *his* unda dehiscens . . .'. The scene of general confusion is illustrated by a series of isolated and representative vignettes. This technique is also characteristic of Roman historians, especially when depicting disordered crowd scenes. Cf. P. G. Walsh, *Livy: His Historical Aims and Methods*, pp. 185-6.

489. *rapit antemnas:* 'rapit' suggests a hasty, violent movement: 'hurriedly lowers the yard-arm'.

491. *bella gerunt venti:* for the description of the storm in terms of a war of the winds, cf. Vergil, *Aeneid* ii. 416–18:

> adversi rupto ceu quondam turbine venti
> confligunt, Zephyrusque Notusque et laetus Eois
> Eurus equis.

492. *nec se . . . ipse fatetur scire:* = 'et fatetur se nescire'.

493. *iubeatve velitve:* the phrase is an echo of a Roman constitutional formula. Cf. Livy xlv. 21, 4: 'vellent iuberentue Rhodiis bellum indici' ('whether it was their will and command . . .').

495–8. Dryden here abandons accurate translation for a fine piece of impressionism:

> The Cries of Men are mix'd with rattling Shrowds;
> Seas dash on Seas, and Clouds encounter Clouds:
> At once from East to West, from Pole to Pole,
> The forky Lightnings flash, the roaring Thunders roll.

In its elegance, rapidity and balance this well renders the spirit, if not the letter, of the original.

497. Brooks Otis remarks that from here until l. 534 the picture is empty of human figures: there is nothing but waves, winds and sky.

videtur: note how with this word (cf. l. 504) and with 'credas' (l. 517), Ovid qualifies the conventional exaggerations already found in Vergil, *Aeneid* i. 102ff. (e.g. 'fluctusque ad sidera tollit', 103; 'his unda dehiscens terram inter fluctus aperit', 106–7). These exaggerations were already so extreme in the Aeneid as to make further development difficult. For the *ne plus ultra* of the literary Storm, see Lucan v. 597ff.

498. *inductas:* the clouds are 'drawn over' the sky and so cover or veil it.

499–501. Ovid enlivens the literary convention by a characteristic evocation of colour ('fulvas . . . concolor . . . nigrior . . . albescit') and sound ('spumisque sonantibus').

501. 'or again spreads out in hissing sheets of white foam'.

502. *his agitur vicibus:* 'is swayed by these changes'.

505. *demissam:* sc. 'puppem'.

507. *fluctu latus icta:* Ehwald reads 'fluctu gravis icta', taking 'fluctu gravis' together (= 'weighed down by the waves'). I prefer 'latus icta', the reading of F and N, and take 'latus' to be an accusative of the 'part affected' after 'icta'.

509. *aries ballistave:* the simile from Roman siege-craft contrasts oddly with the Greek-heroic setting of the story. Anachronistic similes are frequent in Ovid, and may even be found in Ennius and Vergil, e.g. *Aeneid* i. 148–53 (Neptune calming the waves compared to a Roman orator calming the mob).

Golding nicely updates the anachronism:

> The Gallye being stricken gave as great a sownde that tyde
> As did sumtyme the Battelrambe of steele or how the Gonne (=Gun)
> In making battrye to a towne.

510. *sumptis incursu viribus:* 'gathering strength with their attack'.
ire pectore: 'to breast'.

513. *arma:* 'defences', the ship's bulwarks.

514. *cunei:* wedges, driven in to secure the individual planks of the hull, one beneath the other. The joins were caulked with a mixture of pitch and wax.

517–18. Many of Ovid's parallelisms (cf. *Met.* v. 605–6) are simply the equivalent of musical trills. Here, the almost word for word and consonant for consonant similarity, together with the end rhyme, reinforces the effect of confusion between sea and sky.

519. *undis:* the very inappropriateness of the word as applied to rain, emphasises the confusion between sea and sky.

520. *ignibus:* ='sideribus'.

523. *ignes:* the fire of the stars, which seemed to be extinguished (ll. 520–1) is now re-ignited by the fire of the lightning. For the same phrase cf. *Met.* ii. 313; *Fasti* vi. 439; and for the verbal trick, cf. l. 488: 'aequorque refundit in aequor'.

524. *texta:* 'fabric', the interwoven planks of the hull.

525f. In comparing the onslaught by waves on a ship to the attack on a walled city by soldiers, Ovid reverses the simile of Homer who (*Iliad* xv. 381ff., 624ff.) compares an attack by (Trojan) soldiers to an onslaught by waves on a ship.

numero praestantior omni: 'far better than all the number' (of his fellow-soldiers).

526. *defensae:* 'beleaguered'.

530. *decimae . . . undae:* every tenth wave was believed to be particularly large and dangerous. Hence the word 'decimanus' came to denote immensity; the satirist Lucilius reproves a glutton for squandering money on an 'immense sturgeon', 'accipensere decimano'.

534. *haud setius:* Ehwald reads 'haud segnius', a reading supported by most of the MSS. (though O omits the line altogether). However, it is difficult to see how the crew can be said to tremble 'none the less actively (zealously)'. My reading follows Heinsius.

534–6. A further development of the siege simile: the sailors' fear is like that of besieged citizens whose walls are either being undermined or already held by the enemy.

536. *trepidare:* to be taken with 'solet'.

539. Ovid emphasises the confusion of the scene by the rapid succession of short, cinematic images ('hic . . . hic . . . ille . . . hic . . . illi . . .

huic'). This piling-up of isolated detail is a favourite technique of Ovid; cf. the series of isolated miniatures in the description of the Flood, *Met.* i. 293ff. See also note on ll. 488–9 above.

540. *funera quos maneant:* cf. l. 429, note.

541. *quod non videt:* here, as so often in a poetic afterthought, Ovid undercuts the pathos of his own narrative by pursuing fancy to the brink of the preposterous. Throughout the passage that follows, the setting (sea, winds, etc.) is continually allowed to distract from the tragedy itself. Ceyx, for instance, wants to go through all the correct motions such as turning his last gaze towards home (l. 547) and calling on Alcyone (l. 566), but is frustrated by the stage properties (waves, winds).

543. *pignoribus:* i.e. children – the pledges which stand security, so to speak, for the love of husband and wife. Not content with Ovid's two family-minded sailors ('illi ... huic'), Dryden, the moralist, adds another as contrast:

> The covetous Worldling in his anxious Mind
> Thinks only on the Wealth he left behind.

544. *in ore:* on his lips. Cf. l. 562: 'sed plurima nautis in ore est / Alcyone coniunx'.

552. *superstes:* sc. 'est' (= 'superstat'). The wave is seen as proudly ('animosa') standing over its spoils (i.e. the rudder and mast) as a victor bestraddles his defeated enemy. 'A billow proudly pranking up as vaunting of his prey' – Golding.

554. *nec levius quam:* 'as heavily as' (to be taken with 'praecipitata cadit').

556. *ictu:* 'the force of the blow' (Innes).

561. *socerumque patremque:* Aeolus and Lucifer.

562. *plurima:* used adverbially.

564–5. *illius ... optat:* the wish strikes an elegiac note. Cf. *Heroides* ii. 135–6 (Phyllis writing to Demophoon):

> Ad tua me fluctus proiectam litora portent
> occurramque oculis intumulata tuis.

566. *quotiens sinit hiscere fluctus:* a characteristic touch of incongruity. Again Ovid's visual realism leads him to puncture a general effect of dignified pathos: not content with the effective glimpse of Ceyx calling on his wife's name (ll. 562–3), Ovid mercilessly follows his hero into the waves to record his desperate gulps of sea water.

The same disproportionately realistic treatment of the same situation is to be found in Hellenistic poetry. Euphorio (librarian of Antioch c. 221 B.C.) in his *Philoctetes* describes a drowning man as 'bringing up his life as he vomited water, waving his arms above the waves while the brine rinsed his teeth' (J. U. Powell, *Collectanea Alexandrina*, no. 44, p. 38). Cf. Propertius iii. 7, 55–6 (of Paetus): 'flens tamen extremis dedit haec mandata querelis / cum moribunda niger clauderet ora liquor'. The situation seems to have fascinated Ovid. Cf. e.g. *Met.* viii. 229–30 (Icarus drowning):

> oraque caerulea patrium clamantia nomen
> excipiuntur aqua.

Perhaps it was of such passages that the elder Seneca was thinking when he said that Ovid could not leave well alone ('nam et Ovidius nescit quod bene cessit relinquere', *Controversiae* ix. 5, 17). The tone is best rendered by Dryden:

> As often as he can catch a Gulp of Air,
> And peep above the Seas, he names the Fair,
> And even when plunged beneath, on her he raves.
> Murm'ring Alcyone below the waves.

569. *caput:* i.e. 'Ceycis'.

571. *illa luce:* i.e. on the following dawn. For the conceit cf. *Met.* ii. 330–1, where after the death of his son Phaethon, the Sun-god is described as hiding his face for a day in mourning.

(iii) **573–673.** *Summary:* Meanwhile Alcyone, ignorant of these events, is preparing for her husband's return, for which she prays daily at Juno's shrine. The goddess, irked by these prayers for one who is already dead, prepares to let Alcyone know the truth. She sends her messenger Iris to the court of Somnus, the god of sleep, asking him to bring the news to the queen by means of a dream. For this task Somnus chooses his son Morpheus who, disguised as Ceyx, appears to Alcyone and announces his death.

573. *Aeolis interea:* after the storm and stress of the previous episode, Ovid 'cuts' to Alcyone and her homely preoccupations. Like a true Ovidian heroine, Alcyone is thinking of what she is going to wear for her husband's return.

577–8. Golding translates, with picturesque anachronism: 'To all the Goddes devoutly shee did offer frankincense: / But most above them all the Church of Juno shee did sence'.

578. *Iunonis:* Juno was the goddess of marriage ('cui vincla iugalia curae' – Vergil, *Aeneid* iv. 59).

579. *nullus erat:* 'was no more'.

582. *hoc:* 'this last prayer', i.e. 'ut nullam sibi praeferret'.

584. *funestas:* 'polluted'. Until a dead man had been given proper burial, his home and family were regarded as unclean.

arceat: for the present subjunctive in past sequence, cf. *Met.* i. 445.

There is an implicit contrast in these and the preceding lines between the cold, bored indifference of the goddess and the faithful piety of her human suppliant. Alcyone can rely on no divine machinery to protect her, even though she is the daughter of Aeolus: all she has is her human love for Ceyx and yet it is through this that she finally conquers fate itself. The gods are in the end, it is suggested, irrelevant.

585. Iris, like Mercury, is a messenger of the gods. In associating her particularly with Juno, Ovid follows Vergil. See *Aeneid* v. 606, and cf. Ceres' words to Iris in *The Tempest*, iv. 1.76ff.

> 'Hail, many colour'd messenger, that ne'er
> Dost disobey the wife of Jupiter;
> Who with thy saffron wings upon my flowers
> Diffusest honey-drops, refreshing showers:
> And with each end of thy blue bow dost crown
> My bushy acres, and my unshrubb'd down,
> Rich scarf to my proud earth. . . .'

587. *mittat:* jussive subjunctive after 'iube'.

588. *veros narrantia casus:* the distinction between 'true' and 'false' dreams goes back to Homer, *Odyssey* xix. 562-9, where Penelope speaks of two kinds of dreams: those which come through the gate of ivory (and are fulfilled), and those which come through the gate of horn (and remain unfulfilled). This tradition is followed by Vergil in *Aeneid* vi. 893-6.

590. *arcuato:* trisyllabic.

591. *iussi:* a transferred epithet. Translate 'as ordered'.

592ff. *The Cave of Sleep:* This episode of hushed and trance-like fantasy is perfectly situated, providing a restful interlude between the violence of the storm scene and the heightened emotion of Alcyone's final reunion with Ceyx. The episode has many of the characteristics of the epyllion (see introduction): it is to some extent a digression, and the elaborate scene painting follows the pattern of the Hellenistic genre. In describing the court of Somnus, Ovid is able to indulge his gift for fantasy all the more freely because the literary tradition had developed no fixed convention. In Vergil (*Aeneid* vi. 273-84) Sleep is 'death's kinsman', living at the threshold of the underworld, 'on the very jaws of Orcus'; here too are to be found the Dreams ('somnia vana'), clustering under the leaves of a great elm. According to Homer (*Odyssey* xxiv. 12), on the other hand, the Dreams dwell on the edge of Ocean at the gates of the Sun, while in Hesiod (*Theogony* 211ff.) they dwell in Tartarus and are, like Sleep and Death, children of Night. This lack of unanimity in the tradition left Ovid free to pick and choose details from various sources, spiced with an originality of his own. The brilliantly descriptive writing in this passage has fired the imagination of many European poets. For a discussion of several adaptations and translations, see the special appendix.

593. *Somni:* Sleep is personified as a god. Such personifications appear first in the *Theogony* of Hesiod, whose description of the dwelling-place of Sleep and Death (*Theogony* ll. 758–60) is the ultimate source of Ovid's inspiration for this passage. The god Hypnos also appears in *Iliad* xiv. 231ff., where he is persuaded by Hera to put Zeus to sleep so that Poseidon may have a chance to rally the Achaeans. Roman poets were especially fond of personifications, none more so than Ovid. Cf. his descriptions of Hunger (*Met.* viii. 801ff.), Envy (ii. 760ff.), and Rumour (xii. 39ff.). The fact that the Romans built temples to deified ideas such as Fides and Concordia no doubt made such personifications seem natural, but Ovid's personifications are no mere abstractions; Somnus, for example, the most successful of all, incorporates the very essence of sleepiness in live detail. Brooks Otis remarks that the remoteness of Somnus' court is emphasised by the fact that he is reached by an intermediary (Iris) and acts by an intermediary (Morpheus).

596. *dubiaeque crepuscula lucis:* 'and a gloaming of twilight'.

597. Notice how the repeated 'i' sound, added to the two hard initial 'c's, echoes the clear, piercing notes of cock-crow.

599. *sagacior anser:* the epithet *sagax*, applied to dogs, means 'keen-scented'. Here, transferred to geese, it refers no doubt to their sense of hearing or, more generally, to their vigilance. For geese as sentries, cf. *Met.* viii. 684 where Philemon and Baucis offer to sacrifice their only goose, 'minimae custodia villae'. Geese had a name for vigilance among the Romans because of the story of how they saved the Capitol from capture by the Gauls. Cf. Livy v. 47, 4.

603. The river Lethe, whose waters induce forgetfulness, flows through the underworld (cf. *Aeneid* vi. 705) and so is only found here, in Cimmerian territory, by poetic licence.

603–4. Here, sound is perfectly wedded to sense. Compare the gentle use of 'crepitantibus' (= 'chattering') with the violence of *Met.* i. 143: 'sanguineaque manu crepitantia (= 'clashing') concutit arma'.

The sound of running water was regarded by the Romans as sleep-inducing. Seneca, in his treatise on Providence (*Dialogues* i. 3, 10), mentions 'aquarum fragores' among the cures for insomnia vainly tried by Maecenas. Cf. Celsus (the encyclopaedist and younger contemporary of Ovid), *de Medicina* iii. 18: 'confert etiam aliquid ad somnum silanus (a fountain) iuxta cadens'.

605. *fecunda:* 'the poppy was so called on account of the abundance of seeds in its pod' (Davies).

608. Ehwald reads 'ianua nec verso stridores cardine reddit': I prefer the reading 'ne . . . reddat' attested by Planudes and adopted by Jahn, which gives more point. As Brooks Otis remarks: 'the squeak of doors is eliminated by the simple expedient of leaving them off'.

610. *ebeno:* 'of ebony' (ablative of description).

614. *somnia vana:* cf. Milton, *Il Penseroso:* 'hovering dreams, the fickle pensioners of Morpheus' train'.

614–15. *quot . . . harenas:* Ovid's similes often go in threes. Cf. *Met.* ix. 498–9.

618. *iacentes:* 'drooping'.

618–20. A supreme example of Ovid's mastery of closely observed detail, laced with humour.

621. *excussit tandem sibi se:* a characteristic play on words, involving a distinction between Sleep and sleep. Many of Ovid's personification narratives include this trick. Cf. for instance *Met.* viii. 819 (Fames filling Erysichthon with hunger): 'seque viro inspirat'.

622. *cognovit enim:* 'for he recognised her'. Golding misunderstands the word to mean that the god went through the motions of asking the reason for Iris' visit though he already *knew* it ('And though he knew for what she came: he askt her what she meand'). This is to attribute to Somnus an alert deviousness of which he was scarcely capable in his condition.

623. *Somne:* the wheedling repetition of the word and the echoing soft sibilants produce a suitably hypnotic effect. This line is echoed in the opening of Statius' poem to Sleep, *Silvae*, 5.4, though Statius pictures the god as a *young* man: 'iuvenis placidissime divum'.

Lines 623–8 follow a liturgical pattern: first the direct invocation of the god, then the praise of his special attributes and finally the prayer. Cf. the many prayers in the Roman breviary which begin 'Deus, qui . . .'.

627. *Trachine:* locative. Trachis is called 'Herculean' because it was the dwelling-place of Hercules in his last years.

628. *adeant:* jussive subjunctive. Cf. l. 587, 'mittat'.

simulacraque naufraga fingant: 'impersonate his ship-wrecked ghost'.

630. Iris hurries away before the prevailing drowsiness of Somnus' court can overcome her. Cf. *Met.* viii. 809–13, where the mountain nymph sent by Ceres on a similar errand to Fames stays only so long as it is necessary to deliver her message, as she can feel the pangs of hunger beginning to affect her.

soporis vim: almost an oxymoron.

634. *artificem simulatoremque:* hendiadys, 'skilled imitator'.

635. *Morphea:* Morpheus (from the Greek μορφή: shape) is, like Icelos (ἴκελος: like), Phobetor (φοβήτωρ: terrifier), and Phantasos, a dream-name invented by Ovid. The name is jauntily abbreviated by Golding: 'Among a thousand sonnes and mo that father Slomber had / He called up Morph, the feyner of mannes shape, a craftye lad'.

636. *sonumque loquendi:* 'tone of voice'.

640. The idea that the same person or thing can have two names, one used by men and the other by the gods, is first found in Homer and Hesiod. In some cases the 'divine' name may have been an archaic word whose original meaning had become obscure.

644. *hi:* i.e. Morpheus, Icelos, Phantasos. Magnus reads *hic* (i.e. Morpheus) . . . *solet,* notwithstanding the awkwardness of making *hic* refer to someone last mentioned six lines back.

645. *populos . . . plebemque:* It is characteristic of Ovid that he should make even his dreams conform to class distinctions. Cf. the description of upper, middle and lower class gods in *Met.* i. 168ff. Dryden, in his rendering, uses the imagery of the theatre:

> These three to Kings and Chiefs their Scenes display,
> The rest before th' ignoble Commons play.

646. *hos:* refers to 'alii' (l. 645).

647. *Thaumantidos:* a Greek genitive; 'of Iris', the daughter of Thaumas.

650. Dryden expands brilliantly:

> Darkling the demon glides for Flight prepar'd,
> So soft that scarce his fanning Wings are heard.

651–2. *urbem . . . Haemoniam:* Trachis.

656. *fluere unda:* sc. 'videtur'.

662. *falso . . . noli:* 'do not cherish false hopes of my return', 'falso' is an adverb.

666. *impleruntfluctus:* cf. note on l. 566.

669. *lugubria:* sc. 'vestimenta'.

670. *indeploratum:* the spondee reinforces the dolefulness of the words. 'Tartara' is baptised by Golding as 'Limbo'.

673. *manus:* nominative.

(iv) 674–748. *Summary:* Alcyone wakes up, and distractedly looks around for her husband, only to break into a passion of grief. The next morning, on going down to the shore to recall her last glimpses of Ceyx, she sees a corpse out at sea. As it gradually approaches with the tide, she moves from doubt to final recognition of her husband's body. She runs out along the harbour mole towards it, and at that moment is changed into a bird. The pitying gods change husband and wife into halcyons, the bringers of calm weather.

674. There is a textual problem here. Ehwald reads 'ingemit Alcyone; lacrimas movet atque lacertos', taking the second half of the line as a zeugma ('bursts into tears and moves her arms'). 'Lacrimas movere', however, means to provoke tears rather than to produce them. I would prefer to read 'ingemit Alcyone lacrimans, movet atque lacertos', but this means that the 'atque' is not only unelided but postponed. Unelided 'atque' is rare in the *Met.* (see the percentages given by M. Platnauer in *Classical Quarterly* 1948, p. 91), and it is almost unknown at the beginning of the fifth foot. The only other example in Ovid of a postponed 'atque' is at *Ars Amatoria* iii. 282 (where the text has been questioned). Heinsius deletes ll. 674–6 altogether, accepting the variant 'sui' for 'sua' in l. 677, so that Alcyone is aroused by her *husband's* voice. I find this less pointed than that she should be woken by her *own* voice (cf. *Met.* i. 638 – of Io). In the circumstances, Gronovius' conjecture 'motatque' makes the best sense of the lines as they stand.

678. Note how the chopped wording echoes Alcyone's agitation. For the effect, cf. *Tristia* iii. 9, 12 (the cry of a look-out as he sights the approach of the Argo): 'Hospes', ait, 'nosco, Colchide, vela, venit'.

679. *nam:* Ovid, like a good stage manager, has not forgotten that it is night and so a lamp must be provided for Alcyone's search. Hence the explanation.

684. *occidit una cum Ceyce suo:* Underlying Alcyone's words there is an implicit syllogism: 'Ceyx and I are one. Ceyx is dead. Therefore I am dead'. This theme, already anticipated (see note on l. 388) finds its ultimate expression in l. 701.

692. *hoc:* deictic. Alcyone points to the spot.

694. *animo . . . divinante:* cf. *Hamlet,* Act i. Sc. 5: 'O my prophetic soul!'

695. *fugeres . . . sequerere:* note how Alcyone continually reverts to the second person in speaking of Ceyx. It is as if no-one else existed for her.

697. *multum fuit utile:* 'it would have been very fitting'.

699. *non simul:* 'apart'.
nec mors discreta fuisset: 'nor would we have been divided in death'.

700–1. A good example of an Ovidian paradox pursued to verbal breaking point. Alcyone and Ceyx are as one in their mutual love (cf. l. 388: 'animasque duas ut servet in una'), so that in a sense when Ceyx dies, Alcyone dies too (cf. ll. 684–5: 'occidit una cum Ceyce suo'). Though far from her husband ('absens'), she is with him 'in spirit' as we would say – tossed on the waves. The sea at once claims her (in so far as she is one with Ceyx) and cannot claim her (in so far as she is herself). The final words 'sine me me pontus habet' are Heinsius' inspired emendation of the MSS. reading 'sine me te'. To say 'the sea holds you without me' is merely trite, whereas to say 'the sea holds me though I am not there' completes the fanciful union/separation motif which Ovid has been developing. This is the most extreme example of a type of word-play to which Ovid was addicted. Cf. *Met.* viii. 862–3 where Erysichthon's daughter, changed into a fisherman, is asked for her own whereabouts by her pursuing master: 'a se se quaeri gaudens'.

706. i.e. though the ashes of husband and wife will not lie in the same urn (since Ceyx' body is lost), yet their names will be juxtaposed in the inscription over their monument: 'Alcyone Ceycis coniunx'.

710. *mane erat:* with cinematic technique Ovid 'cuts' to his climactic scene.

711f. Ovid makes it seem natural and altogether fitting that Alcyone should choose to visit the sea-shore, there to revive her last memories of the living Ceyx. Alcyone's physical surroundings only impinge on her in so far as they are associated with Ceyx (cf. ll. 472–3).

712–13. *hic ... hoc:* deictic, as Alcyone points to the spot.

715–25. How well Ovid manages the transition from Alcyone's first vague glimpse of the distant, unidentified object ('nescio quid quasi corpus'), to the final recognition, thereby reversing the earlier description (ll. 461–73 above) of Ceyx gradually disappearing from view.

719. *ignorans:* concessive.

omine: the (evil) omen consisted in the fact that what the sea first presented to her view was a corpse.

721. *si qua est coniunx tibi:* i.e. 'et misera coniunx, si qua est tibi'.

723. Ehwald reads 'hoc minus et minus est mentis sua': 'the less she is in possession of her mind', justifying this interpretation of 'mentis sua' on the analogy of 'compos mentis', 'inops mentis', etc. Unconvinced by the parallels, I prefer Heinsius' emendation 'amens sua': 'the less the deranged woman is in possession of herself'.

730. *praedelassat:* a compound of Ovidian invention. The prefix 'prae-' suggests that the mole softened the blows of the waves before they reached the shore.

731. *insilit:* the word suggests a bird-like movement (cf. Lesbia's pet bird, 'circumsiliens modo huc modo illuc', Catullus iii. 9), and so contains a hint of what is to come. It is by such means that Ovid makes the moment of metamorphosis both natural and inevitable.

mirumque fuit potuisse: a recurrent theme in Ovid's accounts of metamorphosis. As the humans begin to act like the creatures into which they are gradually being turned, they are amazed at their new-found powers: the mind remains human, observing the changes of the body with wonder and disbelief. Cf. *Met.* iii. 199 (Actaeon): 'et se tam celerem cursu miratur in ipso'. A precedent can be found in Homer's description of Circe's victims (*Odyssey* x. 239–40), who 'had pigs' heads and bristles, and they grunted like pigs; but their minds were as human as they had been before'.

734. *maesto:* sc. 'sono'. Translate: 'her thin chattering beak gave out a plaintive sound like a lament'.

736. *sine sanguine:* for the adjectival phrase (='exsangue') cf. *Met.* viii. 518, 'ignavo ... et sine sanguine leto'.

739. *senserit:* supply 'utrum' (dependent on 'dubitabat').

740–1. *at ille senserat:* previously, Ovid has allowed us to share in the feelings of Ceyx and Alcyone. At the moment of their metamorphosis we see them from outside, through the eyes of spectators, unsure of what they see; then Ovid himself intervenes to reassure us that the spectators' impression was true. Cf. *Met.* ix. 782 (another miracle scene) for a similar editorial parenthesis: 'visa dea est movisse suas (et moverat) aras'.

741. *tandem superis miserantibus:* the gods, who throughout the storm remained so aloof and pitiless, at last relent and allow Ceyx and Alcyone to be reunited in changed shape. Thus finally the impersonal laws of nature yield to the superior power of individual human love.

742. *alite:* kingfishers. These birds (cf. Pliny, *Natural History* x. 90ff.) were supposed to build their nests and hatch their young on the waves over a period of fourteen (or, according to Ovid, seven) days in winter, during which time the sea remained calm (hence 'halcyon days').

742–3. *fatis obnoxius isdem . . . amor:* 'their love, that was subject to the same fate'.

743. *tunc quoque mansit:* Ovid loves to mark the emotional continuity that underlies physical metamorphosis. Ceyx and Alcyone preserve as kingfishers (birds supposedly noted for their constancy) the love they had as humans.

748. *praestatque nepotibus aequor:* 'and guarantees a (calm) sea for his grandsons'. Alcyone's father Aeolus, conspicuous by his absence in the storm scene, now restrains the winds he failed to control before. Dryden aptly expands on these last two lines:

> Her Sire at length is Kind,
> Calms ev'ry Storm, and hushes ev'ry Wind;
> Prepares his Empire for his Daughter's Ease,
> And for his hatching Nephews smooths the Seas.

749–95: AESACUS.
Ovid appends a similar, but briefer, story of 'ornithological' metamorphosis. He manages the transition by means of an imaginary spectator who, seeing Ceyx and Alcyone in flight, is moved to relate another tale of royalty changed into bird-shape by pitying gods. Note the artfulness with which Ovid feigns uncertainty about the identity of the narrator (l. 751, 'proximus aut idem, si fors tulit'). Chronologically, Ovid has now reached the Trojan Age: Peleus, the father of Achilles, has already made his appearance in the Ceyx story, and now, in Aesacus, we are introduced to the brother of Hector.

Summary: Seeing these kingfishers, an old man recalls another royal metamorphosis. Aesacus, the son of Priam and Alexirhoe, threw himself down from a rock in his grief at causing the death of Hesperie, daughter of the Trojan river-god Cebren; as he fell, he was changed by Tethys into a diver. For Ovid's source, see l. 291, note.

751. *si fors tulit:* i.e. 'fortasse'.

752. *gerentem:* translate as 'with'.

753. *spatiosum in guttura:* 'long-throated'. For the use of 'in', cf. *Met.* x. 538: 'celsum in cornua cervum'.

755. *ordine perpetuo:* 'in unbroken line'.

origo: 'forebears'. Ilus, Assaracus, and Ganymede were the sons of

Tros. Ilus was the father of Laomedon and hence the grandfather of Priam.

758. *iste:* deictic: 'the bird over there'.

759. Magnus, following N, reads 'qui nisi sensisset'. I prefer Heinsius' reading. For the use of 'cedere' (= 'to fall to the lot of'), cf. *Met.* iv. 532; v. 368.

nova: 'strange'.

761. *quamvis:* has no concessive force here, being used only to balance its clause against the clause that follows (cf. Greek μέν . . . δέ).

illum: Hector, whose mother Hecuba was the daughter of Dymas.

763. *Granicus:* a river that runs through the Troad, the scene of Alexander's victory over Darius in 334 B.C. Here the river is personified, and conventionally horned.

768. *captatam . . . Hesperien:* translate 'Hesperie, whom he had often tried to catch . . .'.

769. *patria . . . ripa:* 'on the banks of her father's stream'. Hesperie was the daughter of the Trojan river-god Cebren.

772. *longeque lacu deprensa relicto:* 'caught far from her own pool' (Innes).

773. *fluvialis anas:* 'a Mallard' – Golding.

775–6. The description of Hesperie's death by snake-bite is modelled on Vergil's account of the death of Eurydice, *Georgics* iv. 457ff.

779. *neque erat mihi vincere tanti:* 'my victory was not worth so great a price'.

780. *nos . . . duo:* i.e. Aesacus and the snake.

784. *Tethys:* the wife of Oceanus, was the mother of Granicus (l. 763) and thus the great-grandmother of Aesacus.

miserata: the metamorphosis is produced by divine pity, as are those of Ceyx and Alcyone (cf. l. 741, 'superis miserantibus') and that of Daedalion (l. 339, 'miseratus Apollo'). This is a characteristic motif of Boeo's *Ornithogonia*, Ovid's probable source. See A. S. Hollis's note on viii. 251–9.

787. *invitum:* sc. 'se'.

obstari: impersonal.

sede: i.e. his body.

791. *levat casus:* 'broke his fall'.

793. *longa internodia crurum:* 'he has long, jointed legs'.

795. *nomen:* i.e. 'mergus', the diver. Cf. Varro, *de Lingua Latina* v. 78: 'mergus dicitur quod mergendo in aquam captat escam'. Such etymologies (often wildly inaccurate) were popular with ancient writers.

APPENDIX I

VARIATIONS FROM THE TEUBNER TEXT

Appended below are those readings of the Teubner text from which I have differed, together with brief indications of the MS. authorities. There is a useful short summary of the MS. tradition of the *Metamorphoses* in the Critical Notes at the end of A. G. Lee's edition of Book i.

M = Marcianus Florentinus 225 (11th cent.), ending at xiv. 830.

N = Neapolitanus (12th cent.), ending at xiv. 838.

F = Marcianus Florentinus 223 (11th or 12th cent.).

L = Laurentianus Florentinus (11th or 12th cent.), ending at xii. 298.

Plan. = A Greek prose translation of the 13th cent. by the Byzantine monk Maximus Planudes.

For Heinsius, see footnote.

Line

22. titulum rapuere theatri;
    theatri, M N L. triumphi, Plan., Merkel.

26. cum matutina.
    cum, M F. ceu, Heinsius.

45. tua carmina.
    tua, M N L. te, Bentley.

138. perque iugum Lydum.
    iugum ripae, N F, Magnus. iugum Lydum, Ehwald.

167. instrictam.
    instrictam, M. instructam, N L.

180. turpisque.

turpique, M N.   turpisque, Magnus.

293. tantum.

tantum, M N.   iam tum, Magnus.

319. progenitore Tonanti.

tonanti, M.   tonante, N.   nitenti, Bentley.

366. mucisque palustribus.

niveisque paludibus, M.

silvisque palustribus, N.

mucisque palustribus, Merkel.

iuncisque palustribus, Korn.

393. nota grata.

loca grata, M N.   nota grata, Madvig.

456. armarique.

armarique, M N.   aptarique, Magnus.

507. gravis icta.

gravis, M.   latus, N F.

510. incursus.

incursus, M.   incursu, N.

534. haud segnius.

segnius, codd.   secius, Heinsius.

538. veniant.

veniant, M.   veniunt, N.

608. ianua nec verso stridores cardine reddit.

nec ... reddit, N(2).   ne ... reddit, M N(1).

ne ... reddat, L, Plan.

611. atricolor.

atricolor, Heinsius.   unicolor, N.

atque color, M.

635. illo.

illo, L N(2).   illic, M.

644–5. hic ... solet.

hic ... solet, M.   hi ... solent, Plan., Heinsius.

674. ingemit Alcyone; lacrimas movet atque lacertos.

lacrimas, N.   lacrimans, Naugerius.

motatque, Gronovius.

692. ipso.

 ipso, N. ipse, M, Magnus.

723. hoc minus et minus est mentis sua, iamque propinquae.

 mentis sue, N. mentis suae, M. mentis sua,
 Magnus.

 amens sua, Heinsius, Burman.

Footnote. Many of the more inspired emendations of Ovid's
text are the work of the scholar N. Heinsius, several times
referred to in the text. Heinsius (1620–1681) was a Dutch
statesman, adviser to Queen Christina of Sweden, who in
the course of his diplomatic journeys made an extensive
study of classical MSS., particularly of the Latin poets. To
his edition of Ovid he brought remarkable taste and
judgment (N.B. his emendation at xi. 701). He was himself
an accomplished writer of Latin elegy; among his Latin
poems was a eulogy of General Monk (Duke of Albemarle),
the restorer of the Stuarts.

APPENDIX II

SOME ENGLISH ADAPTATIONS
AND TRANSLATIONS OF *MET.* XI, 592–615

1. John Gower, *Confessio Amantis*, iv. 2991–3022.

Gower was a contemporary and friend of Chaucer. The *Confessio* (c. 1390), which takes the form of a lover's confession to Genius, the priest of Venus, provides him with a framework within which to include many stories from classical and medieval sources. He adapts Ovid to his own purposes here, adding many details of his own.

> Under an hell ther is a cave,
> Which of the Sonne mai noghte have,
> So that noman mai knowe ariht
> The point between dai and nyht:
> Ther is no fyr, ther is no sparke,
> Ther is no dore which mai charke,
> Whereof an yhe scholde unschette,
> So that inward ther is no lette.
> And forto speke of that withoute,
> Ther stant no gret Tree nyh aboute
> Wher on ther myhte crowe or pie
> Alihte, forto clepe or crie:
> Ther is no cok to crowe day,
> Ne beste non which noise may
> The hell, bot al aboute round
> Ther is growende upon the ground
> Popi, which berth the sed of slep,
> With othre herbes suche an hep.
> A stille water for the nones
> Rennende upon the smale stones,

> Which hihte of Lethes the rivere,
> Under that hell in such manere
> Ther is, which yifth gret appetit
> To slepe. And thus full of delit
> Slep has his hous; and of his couche
> Withinne his chambre if I schal touche,
> Of hebenus that slepi tree
> The bordes al aboute be,
> And for he scholde slepe softe,
> Upon a fethrebed alofte
> He lith with many a pilwe of doun:
> The chambre is strowed up and doun
> With swevenes many thousenfold.

charke = creak	pie = magpie
yhe = eye; unschette = open	hihte = is called
lette = hindrance	swevenes = dreams

2. From Arthur Golding's translation, 1567.

Golding's was the first complete translation of the *Metamorphoses* into English verse. A prose rendering of a French translation had been published by William Caxton in 1480. Written in a jaunty metre of fourteen syllables to the line, Golding's version makes up for what it lacks in subtlety, polish, and economy by its gusto and good humour. The author succeeds in thoroughly 'Englishing' the atmosphere of the *Metamorphoses*, peopling its world with apple-cheeked wenches and merry peasants. Even the religion is brought up to date, so that Juno's temple, for instance, becomes a 'church', Bacchantes become 'nuns of Bacchus' and Orpheus a 'chaplain' of Bacchus' 'orgies'. Names are abbreviated with affectionate familiarity to Orphey, Penthey, Morph and even Thisb. Most engaging of all to a modern ear is Golding's highly flavoured vocabulary. While Ezra Pound's praise ('the most beautiful book in the language' – *ABC of Reading*) is over-shrill, it is certainly a relief to turn to Golding from the more accurate but relatively colourless style of translation that is current today. Above all, Golding makes Ovid enjoyable. See the excellent introduction by his latest editor, Professor J. F. Nims.[1]

Among the darke Cimmerians is a hollow mountaine found,
And in the hill a Cave that farre dooth ronne beneath the
    ground,
The chamber and the dwelling place where slouthful sleepe
    dooth cowch;
The lyght of *Phebus* golden beames this place can never
    towch.
A foggye mist with dimness mixt streames upward from the
    ground,
And glimmering twylyght evermore within the same is
    found.
No watchfull bird with barbed bill and combed crowne
    doothe call
The morning foorth with crowing out. There is no noyse at all
Of waking dogge, nor gagling goose more waker than the
    hound,
Too hinder sleepe. Of beast ne wyld ne tame there is no
    sound
No bowghes are stird with blastes of wynd, no noyse of
    tatling toong
Of man or woman ever yit within that bower roong.
Dumb quiet dwelleth there. Yit from the Roches foote dooth
    go
The ryver of forgetfulnesse, which ronneth trickling so
Uppon the little pebble stones which in the channell lye,
That untoo sleepe a great deale more it dooth provoke
    thereby.
Before the entry of the Cave, there growes of Poppye store,
With seeded heades, and other weedes innumerable more,
Out of the milkye jewce of which the night dooth gather
    sleepes,

[1] See bibliography, Appendix III.

And over all the shadowed earth with dankish deawe them
    dreepes.
Bycause the craking hindges of the doore no noyse should
    make,
There is no doore in all the house, nor porter at the gate.
Amid the Cave, of *Ebonye* a bedsted standeth hye,
And on the same a bed of downe with keeverings black dooth
    lye
In which the drowzye God of sleepe his lither limbes dooth
    rest.
About him, forging sundrye shapes as many dreames lye
    prest,
As eares of corne doo stand in feeldes in harvest tyme, or
    leaves
Doo grow on trees, or sea too shore of sandye cinder heaves.'

3. George Sandys's Translation (1621. Revised edition,
    1632).

Sandys composed some of his translation in America,
where he was the colonial treasurer of the Virginia Company.
He chose the heroic couplet as his medium, and in this prepared the ground for poets like Dryden and Pope, greatly
influencing their taste and technique. As far as possible he
made his lines correspond with those of Ovid; sometimes
this gives a syntactically strained and awkward effect (e.g.
'beasts tame nor salvage' for 'nec fera nec pecudes'), but
at its best his verse has a smoothness, variety, and elegance
worthy of the original. Whereas Dryden's lines are self-
contained sense units, Sandys, like Ovid himself, lets one
line run on into another. The resulting verse is relaxed and
varied.

> Neere the Cimmerians lurks a Cave, in steepe
> And hollow hills, the Mansion of dull Sleepe:
> Not seene by *Phoebus* when he mounts the skies,
> At height, nor stooping: gloomie mists arise
> From humid earth, which still a twilight make.

No crested fowles shrill crowings here awake
The chearfull Morne: no barking Sentinell
Here guards; nor geese, who wakefull dogs excell.
Beasts tame, nor salvage; no wind-shaken boughs,
Nor strife of jarring tongues, with noyses rouse
Secured Ease. Yet from the rock a spring,
With streames of *Lethe* softly murmuring,
Purles on the pebbles, and invites Repose.
Before the entry pregnant Poppie grows,
With numerous Simples; from whose juicie birth
Night gathers sleepe, and sheds it on the earth.
No doores here on their creeking hinges jarr'd:
Throughout this court there was no doore, nor guard.
Amid the *Heben* cave a downie bed
High mounted stands, with sable coverings spred.
Here lay the lazie God, dissolv'd in rest.
Fantastick Dreames, who various formes exprest,
About him lay: than Autumn's leaves far more,
Or leaves of trees, or sands on *Neptunes* shore.

4. Edmund Spenser, *The Faerie Queene* (1579–1594), Book I,
   Canto I, 39–41.

This is not a translation, but an adaptation in which
Spenser conflates details from Ovid and other sources, including Homer, Vergil, Statius, Chaucer and the Italian
Ariosto. With these materials he creates something entirely
his own. He makes free with the tradition; for instance,
Morpheus is not one of the sons of Sleep, as in Ovid, but
Sleep himself, and where Ovid admits of no sound but a
trickling stream, Spenser adds 'ever-drizling raine' and
'a murm'ring winde, much like the sowne of swarming
bees' – details which with their subtly soporific effect
improve on the Ovidian original. These stanzas provide
the best example of how one writer's inspiration can liberate
and nourish the imagination of another. The Ovidian spirit
can assume many shapes.

He, making speedy way through spersed ayre,
And through the world of waters wide and deepe,
To Morpheus house doth hastily repaire.
Amid the bowels of the earth full steepe,
And low, where dawning day doth never peepe,
His dwelling is; there Tethys his wet bed
Doth ever wash, and Cynthia still doth steepe
In silver deawe his ever-drouping hed,
Whiles sad night over him her mantle black doth spred.

Whose double gates he findeth locked fast,
The one faire fram'd of burnisht Yvory,
The other all with silver overcast;
And wakeful dogges before them farre doe lye,
Watching to banish Care their enemy,
Who oft is wont to trouble gentle Sleepe.
By them the sprite doth passe in quietly,
And unto Morpheus comes, whom drowned deepe
In drowsie fit he finds: of nothing he takes keepe.

And more to lull him in his slumber soft,
A trickling streame from high rock tumbling downe,
And ever-drizling raine upon the loft,
Mixt with a murm'ring winde, much like the sowne
Of swarming bees, did cast him in a swowne.
No other noyse, nor peoples troublous cryes,
As still are wont t'annoy the walled towne,
Might there be heard; but carelesse Quiet lyes
Wrapt in eternall silence farre from enimyes.

5. John Dryden: 'Ceyx and Alcyone', in *Fables, Ancient and Modern* (1700), xi. 268–99.

Dryden was no uncritical admirer of Ovid, but where Ovid is at his best, Dryden responds with equal inspiration, bringing to his task that urbanity (in both senses of the word) which is common to both poets. The couplets are more elegant than those of Sandys, but the correspondence of rhyme ending with sense ending breaks up the narrative flow. It is noticeable, too, how Dryden, partly by his choice of words ('Mansion', 'palace', 'plains', 'house'), partly by his insertion of formal epithets ('dark' abode, 'gloomy' mansion, 'perpetual' twilight, 'crowing' cock, 'sweet' rest, etc.) slightly freezes the Ovidian picture. Each separate detail is balanced against the rest, but there is a corresponding lack of freedom. But in stately dignity Dryden is unsurpassed.

> Near the *Cymmerians*, in his dark Abode
> Deep in a Cavern, dwells the drowzy God;
> Whose gloomy Mansion nor the rising Sun
> Nor setting visits, nor the lightsome Noon:
> But lazy Vapors round the Region fly,
> Perpetual Twilight, and a doubtful Sky;
> No crowing Cock does there his Wings display
> Nor with his horny Bill provoke the Day:
> Nor watchful Dogs, nor the more wakeful Geese,
> Disturb with nightly Noise the sacred Peace:
> Nor Beast of Nature, nor the tame are nigh,
> Nor Trees with Tempests rock'd, nor human Cry.
> But safe Repose without an air of Breath
> Dwells here, and a dumb Quiet next to Death.
>   An arm of *Lethe* with a gentle flow
> Arising upwards from the rock below,
> The Palace moats, and o'er the Pebbles creeps,
> And with soft Murmers calls the coming Sleeps:
> Around its entry nodding Poppies grow,
> And all cool Simples that sweet Rest bestow;
> Night from the Plants their sleepy Virtue drains,
> And passing sheds it on the silent Plains:
> No Door there was th'unguarded House to keep,
> On creaking Hinges turn'd, to break his Sleep.
>   But in the gloomy Court was raised a Bed
> Stuff'd with black Plumes, and on an Ebon-Sted:
> Black was the covering too, where lay the God

And slept supine, his Limbs display'd abroad:
About his head fantastick Visions fly,
Which various Images of Things supply,
And mock their Forms, the Leaves on Trees not more;
Nor bearded Ears in Fields, nor Sands upon the Shore.

6. Translation by Rolfe Humphries (1955), Indiana
   University Press.

Far down, under a Cimmerian mountain,
A cavern winds, the home of lazy Sleep,
His dwelling-place and shrine. No sunlight ever
Comes there at morning, noon, or evening, only
A dubious twilight, and the ground is dark
With mist, and the fog settles there. No bird
With clarion cry ever calls out the morning,
Dogs never break the silence with their barking,
Geese never cackle, cattle never low,
No boughs move in the stir of air, no people
Talk in their human voices. Only quiet.
From under the rock's base a little stream,
A branch of Lethe, trickles with a murmur
Over the shiny pebbles, whispering Sleep!
Before the doors great beds of poppies bloom
And other herbs, whose juices night distils
To sprinkle Slumber over the darkened earth.
There is no door to turn upon its hinge
With jarring sound, no guardian at the gate.
But in the very center, a dark couch
Rises on ebony framework, all one color,
Downy and soft, and with a counterpane
Of black thrown over it. Here the god is lying,
Dissolved in slumber. And around him lie
In various forms, the unsubstantial dreams,
As numerous as the wheat-ears of the harvest,
The green leaves of the woods, or grains of sand
Along the shore.

If Ovid is to be robbed of his poetry, one may at least
expect some compensating precision of language in a
translation, but even this is lacking here. Where, for instance,
is 'convicia' in the curious rendering 'no people / talk in
their human voices'? One hopes that 'shiny' is not meant to
be a translation of 'crepitantibus', and that 'great beds of
poppies' are not deduced from 'fecunda'. (Surely no-one
at Somnus' court had the energy for gardening?) Mr
Humphries' own interpolated details are not enlivening.
Cattle, for instance, 'never low', the stream is 'little' and
the leaves are 'green'. It is a pity that the translator should
father such tired expressions onto so fastidious a poet as
Ovid.

APPENDIX III

SELECT BIBLIOGRAPHY

ALBRECHT, M. von, 'Ovids Humor und die Einheit der Metamorphosen', in *Atti del Convegno Internazionale Ovidiano*, 1958.

BERNBECK, E. J., *Beobachtungen zur Darstellungsart in Ovids Metamorphosen*. Munich, 1967.

CRUMP, M. M., *The Epyllion from Theocritus to Ovid*. Blackwell, 1931.

DAVIES, G. A. T., *Metamorphoses xi*. With introduction and notes. Clarendon Press, 1907.

EHWALD, R., Fourth edition (1916) of vol. 2 (Books viii–xv) of the Haupt–Korn *Metamorphoses* commentary. Fifth edition, with corrections and bibliographical additions by M. von Albrecht. Weidmann, Zürich/Dublin, 1966.

FRÄNKEL, H., *Ovid, a poet between two worlds*. University of California Press, 1945.

FRIEDRICH, W. H., 'Episches Unwetter', in *Festschrift Bruno Snell*, pp. 77–87. Munich, 1956.

GOLDING, A., Translation (1567) of Ovid's *Metamorphoses*, edited, with an introduction and notes, by J. F. Nims. Macmillan Company of New York, 1965.

HOLLIS, A. S., *Metamorphoses viii*. With introduction and commentary. Clarendon Press, 1970.

INNES, M., *The Metamorphoses of Ovid* (a prose translation). Penguin Classics, 1955.

LAFAYE, G., *Metamorphoses*, vol. 2 (books 11–15). Third edition, Paris, 1960.

LEE, A. G., *Metamorphoses i*. With introduction and notes. Cambridge University Press, 1953.

MAGNUS, H., *Metamorphoses*. Berlin, 1914.

MURRAY, G., 'Poiesis and Mimesis', in *Essays and Addresses*, Allen and Unwin, 1921, pp. 107–24.

OTIS, B., *Ovid as an Epic Poet*. Cambridge University Press, 1966.

TRAENKLE, H., 'Elegisches in Ovids Metamorphosen', in *Hermes* 91 (1963), pp. 459–76.

WEGE DER FORSCHUNG XCII, *Ovid*. (Essays by J. Stroux, H. Diller, H. Herter, W. H. Friedrich and others). Darmstadt, 1968.

WILKINSON, L. P., *Ovid Recalled*. Cambridge University Press, 1955.

VOCABULARY

ABBREVIATIONS

abl., ablative.
acc., accusative.
adj., adjective.
adv., adverb.
c., common (gender).
comp., *compar.*, comparative.
conj., conjunction.
dat., dative.
demonstr., demonstrative.
dep., deponent.
dimin., diminutive.
f., feminine.
gen., genitive.
imper., imperative.
imperf., imperfect.
impers., impersonal.
indeclin., indeclinable.
indef., indefinite.
infin., infinitive.
interj., interjection.

interrog., interrogative
irreg., irregular.
lit., literally.
m., masculine.
n., neuter.
neg., negative.
nom., nominative.
part., participle.
pass., passive.
pl., plural.
prep., preposition.
pres., present.
pron., pronoun.
reflex., reflexive.
rel., relative.
semi-dep., semi-deponent.
subj., subjunctive.
subst., substantive.
superl., superlative.
vb., verb.

abdō, -ere, -didī, -ditum, hide.
abeō, -īre, -iī, -ītum, go away; pass.
absēns, *pres. part.* of **absum.**
absīstō, -ere, -stitī, cease.
absum, -esse, āfuī, be away, absent, distant.
ac, *conj.* and
Acastus, -ī, *m.* a king of Thessaly.
accendō, -ere, -dī, -sum, inflame, incite.
accipiō, -ere, -cēpī, -ceptum, accept, receive, harbour.
accipiter, -tris, *m.* hawk, falcon.
ācer, ācris, ācre, *adj.* sharp, fierce, bold.
Acheron, -tis, *m.* a river of Hades; the underworld.
actum, -ī, *n.* a deed.

acūmen, -inis, *n.* point, extremity.

addō, -ere, -didī, -ditum, add.

adeō, -īre, iī, -itum, go to, approach.

adhibeō (2), receive, admit.

adhūc, *adv.* yet, hitherto; still.

adiaceō (2), lie near.

adiciō, -ere, -iēcī, -iectum, add.

adimō, -ere, -ēmī, -emptum, take away.

adloquor, -ī, -locūtus, address.

admissum, -ī, *n.* crime.

admittō, -ere, -mīsī, -missum, allow; (of a horse) give rein to; **se admittere,** to rush headlong, charge.

admoneō (2), remind.

admoveō, -ēre, -mōvī, -mōtum, bring near, put to, apply.

adnuō, -ere, -uī, -ūtum, nod in assent, grant.

adōrō (1), worship; pray to, beg.

adscendō, -ere, -dī, -sum, climb, mount.

adscensus, -ūs, *m.* ascent.

adsiliō, -īre, -siluī, -sultum, leap or spring on.

adspergō, -inis, *f.* spray.

adspiciō, -ere, -spexī, -spectum, behold, see.

adstō, -stāre, -stitī, stand at, near.

adstringō, -ere, -inxī, -ictum, tighten.

adsuescō, -ere, -suēvī, -suetum, accustom, be accustomed.

adsum, -esse, -fuī, be present; (+ *dat.* stand by).

adsūmō, -ere, -sumpsī, -sumptum, take, receive, put on.

aduncus, -a, -um, *adj.* curved, hooked.

adventus, -ūs, *m.* coming, arrival.

adversus, -a, -um, *adj.* facing, opposite; contrary, hostile.

advolō (1), fly to, speed to.

Aeacides, -ae, *m.* son of Aeacus, i.e. Peleus.

aedificō (1), build.

Aegaeus, -a, -um, *adj.* Aegean.

Aeolis, -idis, *f.* daughter of Aeolus, i.e. Alcyone.

aequālis, -e, *adj.* regular, measured.

aequō (1), equal, match; reach, touch.

aequor, -oris, *n.* sea.

aequoreus, -a, -um, *adj.* of the sea.

aequus, -a, -um, *adj.* kind, favourable, well-disposed.

āēr, āeris (*acc.* **āera**), *m.* air.

Aesacos, -ī, *m.* son of Priam by Alexirhoe (*acc.* **Aesacon**).

aether, -eris, *m.* sky, heaven.

age (*imper.* of **ago**), come!

ager, -grī, *m.* land, field; the country.

agitō (1), drive, chase, harry.

agmen, -inis, *n.* column, train, procession.

agnoscō, -ere, -nōvī, -nitum, recognise, know.

agō, agere, ēgī, actum, drive; do, perform; act upon, impel, sway; **agere festum,** keep holiday

agrestis, -e, *adj.* of the country, rustic, boorish; as *subst.* countryman.

agricola, -ae, *m.* farmer, planter.

āiō, ais, ait, *defective vb.,* say.

āla, -ae, *f.* wing.

albeō (2), be white.

albescō (3), become white.

Alcīdēs, -is, *m.* descendant of Alceus, i.e. Hercules.

āles, ālitis, *c.* bird.

Alexirhoē, -ēs, *f.* daughter of the river-god Granicus, mother of Aesacos.

alga, -ae, *f.* sea-weed.

ālipēs, -pedis, *adj.* with winged feet.

aliquis, -qua, -quid, *indef. pron.,* someone.

aliter, *adv.* otherwise.

alius, -a, -ud, *adj.* other, another. **alii . . . alii,** some . . . others.

alter, -erius, *adj.* other (of two).

altor, -ōris, *m.* foster-father.

altrix, -īcis, *f.* nurse.

alumnus, -ī, *m.* foster-son.

amans, -tis, *c.* (*part.* of **amo**), lover.

ambiguus, -a, -um, *adj.* doubtful, uncertain; untrustworthy.

ambo, -ae, -o, both.

āmens, -ntis, *adj.* distracted.

amīcus, -a, -um, *adj.* friendly.

amnis, -is, *m.* river.

amō (1), love.

amor, -ōris, *m.* love.

amplector, -ī, -plexus, embrace, clasp.

amplius, *compar. adj.,* longer, further.

an, *interrog. conj.* or ?

anas, -atis, *f.* duck.

anguis, -is, *m.* snake.

angustus, -a, -um, *adj.* narrow.

anhēlus, -a, -um, *adj.* breathless, panting.

anima, -ae, *f.* breath, life; ghost.

animōsus, -a, -um, *adj.* spirited, proud.

animus, -ī, *m.* mind, character; feeling, disposition; courage, spirit.

annus, -ī, *m.* year.

anser, -eris, *m.* goose.

ante, *prep.* + *acc.* before, in preference to; *adv.* sooner, before.

ante ... quam, *conj.* before.

anteeō, -īre, -iī, -ītum, go before, precede.

antemna, ae, *f.* yard-arm.

antīquus, -a, -um, *adj.* ancient, former.

antrum, -ī, *n.* cave.

anus, -ūs, *f.* old woman.

anxius, -a, -um, *adj.* distressed, troubled.

aperiō, īre, -uī, -rtum, open.

apertus, -a, -um, *adj.* open.

Apollineus, -a, -um, *adj.* of Apollo. **appello, -ere, -puli, -pulsum,** drive to.

aptō (1), fit, equip.

aqua, -ae, *f.* water.

āra, -ae, *f.* altar.

arbitrium, -iī, *n.* choice, power.

arbor (arbos), -oris, *f.* tree; mast.

arceō (2), keep off; prevent, restrain.

arcuātus, -a, -um, *adj.* curved (like a bow).

arcus, -ūs, *m.* bow, arch. **arcus aquarum,** an arching wave.

ardeō, -ēre, arsī, burn, sparkle.

ardescō, -ere, arsī, sparkle, glitter.

arduus, -a, -um, *adj.* steep, lofty.

āreō (2), be dry, parched.

arguō, -ere, -ui, -ūtum, challenge, call in question.

āridus, -a, -um, *adj.* dry, parching.

ariēs, -etis, *m.* ram; battering-ram.

arista, -ae, *f.* ear of corn.

arma, -ōrum, *n. pl.* arms, implements, equipment.

armāmenta, -ōrum, *n. pl.* tackle, gear.

armentum, -ī, *n.* herd.

ars, artis, *f.* skill.

artifex, -icis, *m.* artist, workman, expert.

artus, -ūs, *m.* limb.

arvum, -ī, *n.* field.

arx, arcis, *f.* fortress; height.

asellus, -ī, *m. dimin.* young ass; donkey.

asper, -era, -erum, *adj.* rough, wild; cruel, infuriated.

Assaracus, -ī, *m.* king of Troy, son of Tros.

ast (at), *conj.* but.

astrum, -ī, *n.* star.

āter, -tra, -trum, *adj.* black.

Athos, -ōnis, *m.* a high mountain in N. Greece.

attonitus, -a, -um, *part.* of **attono,** thunderstruck, amazed.

auceps, -cupis, *m.* fowler.

auctor, -ōris, *m.* originator, cause; giver, source.
audeō, -ēre, ausus, dare, presume to.
audiō (4), hear.
auferō, -ferre, abstulī, ablātum, carry away, take from.
aula, -ae, *f.* court, palace.
aura, -ae, *f.* air, breeze. **efferre sub auras,** bring to light.
aureus, -a, -um, *adj.* golden.
auris, -is, *f.* ear.
Aurōra, -ae, *f.* the goddess of the morning; dawn.
aurum, -ī, *n.* gold.
Auster, -trī, *m.* South wind; wind.
ausum, -ī, *n.* crime, daring deed or purpose.
aut, *conj.* either, or.
Autolycus, -ī, *m.* son of Chione by Mercury.
auxilium, -iī, *n.* aid; armed support.
avārus, -a, -um, *adj.* covetous, miserly, mean.
avidus, -a, -um, *adj.* greedy, eager.
avis, avis, *f.* bird.
avus, -ī, *m.* grandfather, ancestor.

bāca, -ae, *f.* berry.
Bacchae, -ārum, *f. pl.* Bacchantes, women followers of Bacchus.
Baccheus, -a, -um, *adj.* of Bacchus.
Bacchus, -ī, *m.* the god of wine; (by metonymy) wine.
ballista, -ae, *f.* a siege engine used for hurling heavy stones.
barba, -ae, *f.* beard.
barbaricus, -a, -um, *adj.* foreign, uncouth, outlandish.
beātus, -a, -um, *adj.* blessed, happy.
bellum, -ī, *n.* war, fighting.
bēlua, -ae, *f.* beast, monster.
Berecyntius, -a, -um, *adj.* of Berecyntus, a mountain in Phrygia, sacred
    to Cybele.
bicolor, -ōris, *adj.* of two colours.
bicornis, -e, *adj.* two-horned.
bis, *adv.* twice.
bōs, bovis, *c.* cow or bull; cattle.
bracchium, -iī, *n.* arm.
brevis, -e, *adj.* short.
buxus, -ī, *f.* box tree (pale yellow in colour).

cadō, -ere, cecidī, cāsum, fall; set; droop, fail.
caecus, -a, -um, *adj.* blind, dark, unseen.
caedes, -is, *f.* bloodshed, slaughter.
caelestis, -e, *adj.* of or from heaven, heavenly.

caelum, -ī, *n.* heaven.

caeruleus, ⎫ **-a, -um,** *adj.* dark-blue; dark.
caerulus ⎭

calamus, -ī, *m.* reed, pipe.

cālīgo, inis, *f.* gloom, darkness.

callidus, -a, -um, *adj.* cunning, crafty.

calor, -ōris, *m.* heat, passion.

campus, -ī, *m.* field, plain; stretch (of land, water).

candens, -ntis, *adj.* white.

candidus, -a, -um, *adj.* white.

canis, -is, *c.* dog.

canna, -ae, *f.* reed, pipe.

canō, -ere, cecinī, cantum, sing, play (on a musical instrument).

cantus, -ūs, *m.* song; (of cocks) crowing.

capessō, -ere, -iī, -ītum, seize, catch up.

capillus, -ī, *m.* hair.

capiō, -ere, cēpī, captum, take, catch, seize; captivate, enchant; take in, hold, contain.

captō (1), try to catch, chase.

caput, -itis, *n.* head.

carbasus, -ī, *f.* fine linen; a white robe; canvas, sail (*irreg. pl.* **carbasa,** *n.*).

carcer, -eris, *m.* prison.

cardo, -inis, *m.* hinge.

careō (2), lack, want, be without.

carīna, -ae, *f.* keel; ship.

carmen, -inis, *n.* song.

Carpathius, -a, -um, *adj.* of Carpathus, an island between Crete and Rhodes, the home of Proteus.

carpō, -ere, -psī, -ptum, pluck, break off; traverse, cover (a distance).

cārus, -a, -um, *adj.* dear, precious.

cāsus, -ūs, *m.* fall; chance, fortune; calamity.

causa, -ae, *f.* cause, reason, grounds.

cautes, -is, *f.* rock, crag.

cavus, -a, -um, *adj.* hollow, arching.

Cēbrēnis, -idos, *f.* daughter of the river-god Cebren, Alexirhoe (*acc.* **Cebrenida**).

Cēcropius, -a, -um, *adj.* of Cecrops, Athenian. (Cecrops was the mythical founder and king of Athens).

cēdō, -ere, cessi, cessum, go, retire, pass; fall to one's lot (l. 759).

celer, -eris, -ere, *adj.* swift.

cēlō (1), hide.

celsus, -a, -um, *adj.* high, lofty, uplifted.

cēra, -ae, *f.* wax.

cĕrātus (*part.* of cero), fastened with wax.
Cerēs, -eris, *f.* goddess of agriculture; (by metonymy) corn.
Cereālis, -e, *adj.* of Ceres.
cernō, -ere, crēvi, crētum, see, behold.
certāmen, -inis, *n.* contest.
certē, *adv.* at any rate.
certus, -a, -um, *adj.* fixed, resolved; sure, aware; Certum (certiorem) facere aliquem, to inform someone.
cerva, -ae, *f.* deer.
cervix, -icis, *f.* neck.
cervus, -ī, *m.* stag.
ceterus, -a, -um, *adj.* the remaining.
ceu, *adv.* like.
Cēȳx, -ȳcis, *m.* (*acc.* Cēȳca), king of Trachis.
Chione, -ēs, *f.* daughter of Daedalion.
chorus, -ī, *m.* dance; company, troop, band.
Cicones, -um, *m.* a Thracian tribe.
Cimmeriī, -ōrum, *m.* a mythical tribe, who lived in perpetual darkness.
cingō, -ere, -nxi, -nctum, surround, encircle.
circa, *prep.* + *acc.* around.
circum, *prep.* + *acc.* around.
circumlitus (*part.* of circumlino), smeared, coated.
circumspiciō, -ere, -spexī, -spectum, look around at, look about.
circumstō, -stāre, -stetī, -stitum, stand around, surround.
cithara, -ae, *f.* lute.
citrā, *prep.* + *acc.* on this side of.
clādes, -is, *f.* disaster.
clāmō (1), cry, shout.
clāmor, -ōris, *m.* shout, noise.
Clārius, -a, -um, of Claros, a small town in Ionia famous for its oracle of Apollo.
clārus, -a, -um, *adj.* bright; famous, distinguished.
clīvus, -ī, *m.* slope.
coarguō, -ere, -uī, convict, prove guilty; reveal, betray.
coeō, -īre, -ītum, come together, unite; pair, mate.
coepi, *defect. vb.* begin.
coarceō (2), check, fasten.
coetus, -ūs, *m.* assembly, meeting, throng.
cognoscō, -ere, -ōvī, -itum, learn, know; recognise (570).
cōgō, -ere, ēgī, -actum, drive together; compel, force.
cohaereō, -ēre, -haesī, -haesum, cling to, stick to.
cohors, -rtis, *m.* troop, bodyguard.
collābor, -ī, -lapsus, sink down, fall in a faint.
colligō, -ere, -lēgī, -lectum, gather; infer.

collum, -ī, *n.* neck.

colō, -ere, -uī, cultum, cultivate, practise; worship; frequent, haunt.

colōnus, -ī, *m.* farmer, labourer.

color, -ōris, *m.* colour.

coluber, -brī, *m.* snake.

columba, -ae, *f.* dove.

coma, -ae, *f.* hair; foliage.

comes, -itis, *m.* companion.

comitor (1. *dep.*), accompany, attend.

committō, -ere, -mīsī, -missum, entrust, venture, commit.

commodum, -ī, *n.* benefit, favour.

compleō, -ēre, -ēvī, -ētum, fill, fill up; complete; overwhelm.

concentus, -ūs, *m.* harmony.

concipiō, -ere, -cēpī, -ceptum, conceive.

concitus (*part.* of **concieō**), swift, racing.

concolor, -ōris, *adj.* of the same colour.

concursus, -ūs, *m.* clash, charge, encounter.

concutiō, -ere, -cussī, -cussum, shake; strike together, beat.

condō, -ere, -didī, -ditum, hide, bury.

confiteor, -ērī, -fessus, confess, admit.

coniciō, -ere, iēcī, -iectum, hurl.

coniugiālis, -e, *adj.* marriage, nuptial.

coniugium, -iī, *n.* marriage.

coniunctus (*part.* of **coniungō**), united, matched.

coniunx, -ugis, *c.* husband, wife.

congelō (1), freeze, stiffen.

cōnor (1), try, strive.

consīdō, -ere, -sēdī, -sessum, sit down, hold session.

consilium, -iī, *n.* advice, counsel; plan, resolve.

consistō, -ere, -stitī, -stitum, settle, rest, remain.

consors, -rtis, *c.* brother, sister (*lit.* co-heir).

constantia, -ae, *f.* constancy, consistency.

consuescō, -ere, -suēvī, -suētum, be or grow accustomed.

consuētus (*part.* of **consuesco**), usual.

consulō, -ere, -uī, -tum, consult.

contactus, -ūs, *m.* touch.

contemnō, -ere, -tempsī, -temptum, scorn, despise.

contemptor, -ōris, *m.* scorner.

contineō, -ēre, -uī, -tentum, hold in, check, confine.

contingō, -ere, -tigī, -tactum, touch; fall to one's lot.

contrā, *prep.* + *acc.* against; *adv.* on the other hand, in answer.

cōnūbium, -iī, *n.* marriage, intercourse.

convellō, -ere, -ī, -vulsum, tear in pieces; chew.

convīcium, -iī, *n.* clamour.

coorior, -īrī, -ortus, rise, spring up.
cōpia, -ae, *f.* abundance; means, opportunity, permission.
cor, cordis, *n.* heart.
cornū, -ūs, *n.* horn; bow; (nautical) yard.
corōna, -ae, *f.* crown, garland.
corpus, -oris, *n.* body.
crābro, -ōnis, *m.* hornet.
creātus (*part. of* **creō**), sprung (from), begotten (by).
crēber, -bra, -brum, *adj.* abounding in, thick with.
crēdō, -ere, -didī, -ditum, believe.
crepitō (1), murmur, tinkle, chatter, clatter.
crepusculum, -ī, *n.* twilight.
crescō, -ere, crevī, crētum, grow, increase.
crīmen, -inis, *n.* accusation; crime, guilt.
crīnis, -is, *m.* hair.
cristātus, -a, -um, crested.
crūdēlis, -e, cruel, pitiless.
cruentātus (*part. of* **cruentō**), blood-stained.
cruentus, -a, -um, *adj.* bloody.
crūs, crūris, *n.* leg.
cubitum, -ī, *n.* elbow.
cubō, -āre, -uī, -itum, lie, lie down.
culpa, -ae, *f.* fault, blame.
culpō (1), criticise, find fault with.
cumulus, -ī, *m.* heap; summit.
cūnctus, -a, -um, *adj.* all.
cuneus, -ī, *m.* wedge.
cupīdo, -inis, *f.* desire.
cupiō, -ere, -iī, -ītum, desire, long for.
cūra, -ae, *f.* care, thought; concern, trouble, grief.
cūrō (1), attend to; take trouble to, choose to.
currō, -ere, cucurrī, cursum, run, hasten.
cursus, -ūs, *m.* running, speed; voyage.
curvāmen, -inis, *n.* arch, bow.
curvō (1), bend.
curvus, -a, -um, *adj.* bent, rounded, winding.
custōdiō (4), hold prisoner, guard.
custos, -ōdis, *m.* guard, sentry.
Cyllēnēus, -a, -um, *adj.* of Cyllene, a mountain in Arcadia, birthplace of Mercury.

Daedaliōn, -ōnis, *m.* son of Lucifer, brother of Ceyx, father of Chione.
damnō (1), punish.
damnōsus, -a, -um, *adj.* harmful, ruinous.

damnum, -ī, *n.* loss, hurt.

Danaē, -ēs, *f.* daughter of Acrisius, king of Argos, mother of Perseus.

(daps), dapis, *f.* feast (mostly in *pl.*).

dē, *prep.* + *abl.* from, out of, concerning; (*partitive*) of.

dea, -ae, *f.* goddess.

dēbeō (2), owe; (+ *infin.*) ought.

dēcerpō, -ere, -psī, -ptum, pluck off.

decimus, -a, -um, *adj.* tenth.

dēcipiō, -ere, -cēpī, -ceptum, deceive.

dēdecus, -oris, *n.* disgrace, disfigurement.

dēdūcō, -ere, -xī, -ctum, take off, withdraw; (of sails) unfurl.

dēfendō, -ere, -dī, -sum, defend.

dēfensō (1), (*iterative*) repel, defend.

dēficiō, -ere, -fēcī, -fectum, fail, flag.

dēfīgō, -ere, -xī, -xum, fasten, rivet.

dēgener, -eris, *adj.* unworthy of a father's standards.

dēlāmentor (1), *dep.* lament passionately.

dēlēniō (4), soothe, charm.

Dēlius, -a, -um, *adj.* Delian; (as *subst.*) Apollo, born at Delos, an island in the Cyclades.

Delphī, -ōrum, *m. pl.,* a town in Phocis, famous for its temple and oracle of Apollo.

Delphicus, -a, -um, *adj.* of Delphi.

delphīn, -īnis, *m.* dolphin.

dēmittō, -ere, -mīsī, -missum, lower, let down, cast down.

dēmō, -ere, -mpsī, -mptum, take away.

dēmūgiō (4), fill with bellowing.

dēmum, *adv.* at last.

dēnique, *adv.* at last.

dens, -tis, *m.* tooth, fang; **dens Indus,** ivory.

densus, -a, -um, thick, close.

dēpōnō, -ere, -posuī, -positum, lay down, lay aside.

dēprendō, -ere, -ī, -sum, catch, overtake.

dēscendō, -ere, -dī, -sum, descend.

dēserō, -ere, -uī, -tum, forsake, desert.

dēsīderō (1), long, yearn for.

dēspiciō, -ere, -spexī, -spectum, look down at.

dēsum, -esse, -fuī, be lacking, wanting.

dētrahō, -ere, -traxī, -tractum, pull down.

dētrūdō, -ere, -sī, -sum, drive or thrust down.

deus, -ī, *m.* god.

dexter, -tra, -trum, *adj.* on the right.

dextra, -ae, *f.* right hand.

Diāna, -ae, *f.* goddess of hunting, daughter of Jupiter and Latona.

dīcō, -ere, -xī, -ctum, say; stipulate (213).

dictum, -ī, *n.* word.

diēs, ēī, *c.* day.

differō, -ferre, distulī, dīlātum, postpone, defer.

difficilis, -e, *adj.* hard, troublesome.

digitus, -ī, *m.* finger, toe.

dīlectus (*part.* of dīligō), beloved.

dīmittō, -ere, -mīsī, -missum, give up, forgo.

dīmoveō, -ēre, -mōvī, -mōtum, brush aside, thrust away.

dīnumerō (1), count separately.

dīripiō, -ere, -uī, -reptum, tear off.

dīrus, -a, -um, *adj.* dreadful, terrible.

discēdō, -ere, -cessī, -cessum, depart.

discernō, -ere, -crēvī, -crētum, separate, part, divide.

discutiō, -ere, cussī, -cussum, dispel.

disiciō, -ere, -iēcī, -iectum, tear apart.

dispergō, -ere, -sī, -sum, scatter.

dissimilis, -e, *adj.* unlike.

distō, -stāre, be distant, removed.

diū, *adv.*, for a long time.

dīva, -ae, *f.* goddess.

dīvellō, -ere, -vellī (-vulsī, 38), -vulsum (-volsum), tear apart.

dīversus, -a, -um, *adj.* opposite, separate, different.

dīves, -itis, *adj.* rich.

dīvīnō (1), foresee, foretell.

dīvus, -a, -um, *adj.* divine; (as *subst.*) a god.

dō, dāre, dedī, datum, give, allow; cause, make; put, place; **dare se in mare,** to cast oneself into the sea.

doceō, -ēre, -uī, -ctum, teach.

doctus (*part.* of doceō), skilled, experienced.

doleō (2), grieve.

dolor, -ōris, *m.* grief, sorrow, pain.

dominus, -ī, *m.* master, owner.

domus, -ūs, *f.* house, home.

dōnec, *conj.* until.

dōnō (1), present, bestow.

dōnum, -ī, *n.* gift.

dōtātus (*part.* of dōtō), richly endowed.

Dryas, -adis, *f.* a wood-nymph, Dryad.

dubitō (1), doubt, hesitate.

dubius, -a, -um, *adj.* doubtful, uncertain; faint.

dūcō, -ere, -xī, -ctum, lead; charm; take; prolong.

dulcēdō, -inis, *f.* sweetness (of sound, taste, etc.).

dum, *conj.* while, until.

duplicō (1), double.
dūrus, -a, -um, *adj.* hard.
dux, ducis, *m.* leader, chief.
Dymas, -antis, *m.* father of Hecuba.

ecce, *interj.* behold!
ēdō, -ere, didī, -ditum, make known, announce, tell.
Ēdōnis, -idis, *f. adj.* of the Edoni, Thracian.
ēdūcō, -ere, -xī, -ctum, bring out.
efferō, -ferre, extulī, ēlātum, bring out.
efficiō, -ere, -fēcī, -fectum, bring about, render, make.
effodiō, -ere, fōdī, -fossum, dig up or out.
effugiō, -ere, -fūgī, escape or flee from.
egeō (2), lack, want.
ēgerō, -ere, -gessī, -gestum, carry out, discharge.
ēgredior, iī, -gressus, *dep.* go out, leave.
ēgressus, -ūs, *m.* escape.
ēiciō, -ere, -iēcī, -iectum, cast out or up.
ēligō, -ere, -lēgī, -lectum, choose.
ēlūdō, -ere, -lūsī, -lūsum, elude, deceive.
ēluō, -ere, uī, -ūtum, wash away.
ēmittō, -ere, -mīsī, -missum, send out, let loose; shed.
ēn, *interj.* see!, behold!
enim, *conj.* for.
ēnītor, -ī, -nīsus (nixus), bear (child).
eō, īre, iī, ītum, go; (often of swift movement) rush, charge.
ergō, *adv.* therefore.
ērigō, -ere, -rexī, -rectum, raise.
Erīnys, -yos, *f.* Fury; madness.
ēripiō, -ere, -uī, -reptum, rescue, deliver.
errō (1), wander, stray.
et, *conj.* and; both; also.
etiam, *conj.* besides, also, even.
etiamnum (etiamnunc), *adv.* even now, still.
Eumolpus, -ī, *m.* a legendary bard who settled at Eleusis near Athens.
Eurus, -ī, *m.* the S.E. wind.
Eurydicē, -ēs, *f.* wife of Orpheus.
ēvertō, -ere, ī, -versum, overthrow, overturn.
ēvocō (1), call forth, summon.
exanimis, -e, *adj.* lifeless.
exaudiō (4), hear.
excēdō, -ere, -cessī, -cessum, leave, depart.
exciō (4), rouse, startle.
excipiō, -ere, -cēpī, -ceptum, take, receive, catch.

excitō (1), stir up, arouse.
exclāmō (1), cry out.
excutiō, -ere, -cussī, -cussum, shake out or off.
exeō, -īre, -iī, -ītum, leave, depart; rush out.
exhalō (1), breathe out, exhale.
exhibeō (2), reveal.
expellō, -ere, -pulī, -pulsum, drive out, expel.
expōnō, -ere, -posuī, -positum, expose; put out, land.
exposcō, -ere, -poposcī, require, demand.
exprimō, -ere, -pressī, -pressum, represent, imitate.
exsternātus (*part.* of **exsternō**), dismayed, frightened.
exstinguō, -ere, -nxī, -nctum, crush, destroy, slay.
exstō, -stāre, -stitī, stand out, rise above.
exstruō, -ere, -xī, -ctum, heap up, pile.
exsultō (1), spring up, leap away.
extensus (*part.* of **extendō**), stretching out.
extrā, *adv.* outside.
ēxul, -ulis, *c.* exile.

faciēs, -ēī, *f.* face, appearance, beauty.
faciō, -ere, fēcī, factum, make, do, cause.
factum, -ī, *n.* deed.
falcātus, -a, -um, *adj.* sickle-shaped.
fallāciter, *adv.* deceptively.
fallax, -ācis, *adj.* deceitful, deceptive.
fallō, -ere, fefellī, falsum, deceive.
falsō, *adv.* falsely.
falsus (*part.* of **fallō**), false.
fames, -is, *f.* hunger.
famulus, -ī, *m.* slave, servant.
fateor, -ērī, fassus, *dep.* confess.
fātum, -ī, *n.* fate, destiny; ill-fate, destruction.
fēcundus, -a, -um, *adj.* fertile, prolific.
fēlix, -īcis, *adj.* happy, fortunate.
femur, -oris or **-inis,** *n.* thigh.
fera, see **ferus.**
ferīnus, -a, -um, of a wild animal.
feriō (4), strike, beat.
ferō, ferre, tulī, lātum, bear, bring, offer; get; receive; say, relate; display; tend; happen.
ferox, -ōcis, *adj.* brave, spirited, fierce.
ferreus, -a, -um, *adj.* of iron.
ferrum, -ī, *n.* iron; scissors.

ferus, -a, -um, *adj.* wild, savage; as *subst. m.* or *f.*, wild beast.
ferveō, -ēre, ferbuī, boil, foam, seethe.
fessus, -a, -um, *adj.* weary.
festīnō (1), hasten; make with haste.
festīnus, -a, -um, *adj.* hastening.
festus, -a, -um, *adj.* festal; as *subst. n.*, holiday.
fibra, -ae, *f.* entrails.
fides, -is or **-ium,** *f.* lute.
fides, -eī, *f.* faith, pledge, promise, fulfilment.
fīdūcia, -ae, *f.* confidence.
fīdus, -a, -um, *adj.* trusty, faithful.
figūra, -ae, *f.* shape.
fīlia, -ae, *f.* daughter.
fingō, -ere, finxī, fictum, fashion, represent; imagine.
fīniō (4), bound, limit, end.
fīnis, -is, *c.* end.
flāmen, -inis, *n.* blast, breeze, gale; (of the flute) piping.
flamma, -ae, *f.* flame, fire.
flāvus, -a, -um, *adj.* yellow, golden-haired.
flēbilis, -e, *adj.* plaintive.
flectō, -ere, flexī, flectum, turn, bend; persuade.
fleō, -ēre, ēvī, -ētum, weep, lament.
flētus, -ūs, *m.* weeping, tears.
flōreō (2), bloom.
fluctus, -ūs, *m.* wave, billow.
fluitō (1), flow, trickle; wave, flap.
flūmen, -inis, *n.* river.
fluō, -ere, -xī, -xum, flow, trickle, stream.
fluviālis, -e, *adj.* of a river.
focus, -ī, *m.* fire, beacon.
fodiō, -ere, fōdī, fossum, dig; undermine.
foedus, -eris, *n.* bond, contract.
folium, -iī, *n.* leaf.
fons, -tis, *m.* spring, fount.
fores, -um, *f. pl.*, doors.
foret, *imperf. subj.* of **sum.**
forma, -ae, *f.* shape, appearance, beauty.
fors, -rtis, *f.* chance.
forsitan, *adv.* perhaps.
forte, *adv.* by chance.
fortis, -e, *adj.* strong, brave.
fragmen, -inis, *n.* piece.
fragor, -ōris, *m.* crash, roar, tumult.
frangō, -ere, frēgī, fractum, break.

frāter, -tris, *m.* brother.
frēnātus (*part.* of **frēnō**), bridled.
frequentō (1), crowd, throng.
fretum, -i, *n.* sea, strait.
frīgidus, -a, -um, cold.
frīgus, -oris, *n.* cold, chill; shudder.
frons, -dis, *f.* leaf.
fructus, -ūs, *m.* enjoyment, profit, reward; harvest.
frustrā, *adv.* in vain.
frux, frūgis, *f.* corn, grain (mostly in *pl.*).
fuga, -ae, *f.* flight, exile.
fugiō, -ere, fūgī, fugitum, fly, flee.
fulgor, -ōris, *m.* brightness.
fulmen, -inis, *n.* lightning.
fulmineus, -a, -um, *adj.* lightning; flashing.
fulvus, -a, -um, *adj.* yellow, tawny.
fūmus, -ī, *m.* smoke.
fundō, -ere, fūdī, fūsum, pour, shed.
fūnestus, -a, -um, *adj.* deadly, fatal, mournful; **manus funestas,** hands
   polluted (by death).
fungor, -ī, functus, *dep.* discharge, execute, fulfil.
fūnus, -eris, *n.* funeral, funeral honours.
furiālis, -e, *adj.* insane, maniac.
furō (3), rage.
furor, -ōris, *m.* rage, madness.
furtim, *adv.* secretly, by stealth.
furtum, -ī, *n.* knavery, trick.
fūsilis, -e, *adj.* molten, liquid.
futūrum, -ī, *n.* (*part.* as *subst.*) the future.

Ganymēdes, -is, *m.* son of Tros, carried off by an eagle to be Jupiter's
   cupbearer.
gaudeō, -ēre, gāvīsus, *dep.* rejoice, be glad.
gaudium, -iī, *n.* joy.
geminus, -a, -um, *adj.* twofold, double, two.
gemitus, -ūs, *m.* groan, sigh.
gemma, -ae, *f.* jewel.
gena, -ae, *f.* cheek.
geniāliter, *adv.* merrily, jovially.
genitor, -ōris, *m.* father, begetter.
genitus (*part.* of **gignō**), descended from, born of.
gens, gentis, *f.* nation.
genū, -ūs, *n.* knee.
gerō, -ere, gessī, gestum, carry, bear, wear; do, achieve, wage.

gestus, -ūs, *m.* gesture.
glaeba, -ae, *f.* clod.
glans, -dis, *f.* acorn.
glōria, -ae, *f.* glory, renown.
gradior, -ī, gressus, pace, walk, go.
gradus, -ūs, *m.* step.
Grānīcus, -ī, *m.* a river in Asia Minor; the river god Granicus.
grātia, -ae, *f.* kindness, favour.
grātus, -a, -um, *adj.* pleasing, welcome.
gravis, -e, *adj.* heavy, stout.
gravitas, -ātis, *f.* heaviness.
grex, gregis, *m.* flock.
gurges, -itis, *m.* whirlpool, depths, abyss.
guttur, -uris, *n.* throat.

habeō (2), have, hold; wear.
habitō (1), dwell, inhabit.
Haemonia, -ae, *f.* Thessaly.
Haemonius, -a, -um, *adj.* Thessalian.
haereō, -ēre, haesī, haesum, cling, stick.
hāmus, -ī, *m.* talon, claw.
harēna, -ae, *f.* sand; arena (of an amphitheatre).
harundo, -inis, *f.* reed, pipe; arrow, shaft.
hasta, -ae, *f.* spear.
haud, *adv.* not.
hauriō, -īre, hausī, haustum, hollow out, dig.
hebenus, -ī, *m.* ivory.
Hebrus, -ī, *m.* a river in thrace.
Hector, -oris, *m.* son of Priam, leader of the Trojans.
Hellē, -ēs, *f.* daughter of Athamas and Nephele, drowned in the strait to which she gave her name – the Hellespont.
herba, -ae, *f.* herb, grass, plant.
Herculeus, -a, -um, *adj.* of Hercules.
hēros, -ōis, *m.* hero, demigod.
Hēsionē, -ēs, *f.* daughter of Laomedon, king of Troy.
Hesperides, -um, *f. pl.* the daughters of Atlas, guardians of the orchard with the golden apples.
Hesperiē, -ēs, *f.* daughter of the river-god Cebren.
Hesperius, -a, -um, *adj.* western.
hiātus, -ūs, *m.* open mouth, gaping jaws.
hībernus, -a, -um, *adj.* winter.
hīc, *adv.* here.
hiems, -emis, *f.* storm.

hinc, *adv.* hence; **hinc . . . illinc,** on the one side . . . on the other.
Hippotades, -ae, *m.* son of Hippotas, i.e. Aeolus.
hiscō, -ere, open the mouth; gasp, speak.
homo, -inis, *m.* man.
honor, -ōris, *m.* honour, mark of honour, reward.
horrescō, -ere, horruī, shudder.
hospes, -itis, *m.* guest.
hostīliter, *adv.* like an enemy, fiercely.
hūc, *adv.* hither.
humus, -ī, *f.* ground.
Hypaepa, -ōrum, *n.* Lydian town at the foot of Mt Tmolus.

iaceō (2), lie, lie low; (of the sea) be still, calm.
iactō (1), throw, toss; buffet; vaunt, boast of (l. 153).
iam, *adv.* now, already; with *neg.,* (no) longer.
iamdūdum, *adv.* for a long time now; (with *imper.*) straightway.
iānua, -ae, *f.* door.
ibi, *adv.* there.
Icelos, -ī, *m.* son of Somnus.
ictus, -ūs, *m.* blow, stroke.
Ida, -ae, *f.* mountain near Troy.
idcirco, *adv.* therefore; (with *neg.*) (not) for all that.
iēiūnium, -iī, *n.* fast, hunger.
igitur, *conj.* therefore, then.
ignārus, -a, -um, *adj.* ignorant, unaware.
ignāvus, -a, -um, *adj.* lazy, languid.
ignis, -is, *m.* fire; star; passion, ardour.
ignōrō (1), not to know, be ignorant of.
ignōtus, a, -um, *adj.* unknown; as *subst.* stranger.
īlex, -icis, *f.* ilex, holm-oak.
Iliacus, -a, -um, *adj.* Trojan.
illīc, *adv.* there.
illinc, *adv.* thence.
illūc, *adv.* thither; **illuc et illuc,** hither and thither.
Ilus, -i, *m.* son of Tros, king of Troy.
imāgo, -inis, *f.* image, likeness, appearance; mental picture, thought.
imber, -bris, *m.* shower, rain.
imitor (1), *dep.* copy, imitate.
impar, -aris, *adj.* unequal.
impediō (4), hinder.
impellō, -ere, -pulī, -pulsum, drive; shoot, speed.
imperō (1), command.
impetus, -ūs, *m.* attack, onset, momentum; impulse.

impleō, -ēre, -ēvī, -ētum, fill, complete.

impūnē, *adv.* with impunity, unpunished.

īmus, -a, -um, *adj.* lowest, bottom; as *subst.* **imum, -i,** *n.* depth, bottom

inambitiōsus, -a, -um, *adj.* unpretentious, simple.

inānis, -e, *adj.* empty, vain; unreal, unfulfilled.

incessus, -ūs, *m.* way of walking.

inclīnō (1), bend, turn downwards, roll.

incommendātus, -a, -um, *adj.* unprotected, abandoned.

incrēscō, -ere, -crēvī, -crētum, grow, increase, swell.

incubō, -āre, -cubuī, -cubitum, brood on or over.

incumbō, -ere, -cubuī, -cubitum, bend over.

incursus, -ūs, *m.* charge, onset, assault.

inde, *adv.* thence, then.

indēplōrātus, -a, -um, *adj.* unlamented.

indicium, -iī, *n.* information, disclosure.

indicō (1), show.

indignor (1), *dep.* resent, be angry.

indolescō, -ere, -doluī, grieve, be vexed.

indūcō, -ere, -duxī, -ductum, draw over or across; in *pass.* cover, veil.

induō, -ere, -uī, -ūtum, (*pass.* in middle sense) put on, clothe.

indūrō (1), harden, stiffen.

Indus, -a, -um, *adj.* Indian.

inexpugnābilis, -e, *adj.* impregnable, proof against.

infēlix, -icis, *adj.* luckless.

inferiae, -ārum, *f. pl.* offerings to the dead.

inferior, -ius, *compar. adj.* meaner, worse.

infernus, -a, -um, of the underworld.

inferō, -ferre, -tulī, -lātum, bring in; inflict, deal.

inficiō, -ere, -fēcī, -fectum, stain, dye.

infitior (1) *dep.* withhold, deny, refuse.

infractus (*part.* of **infringō**), bent, curved.

infundō, -ere, -fūdī, -fūsum, pour or throw upon; *pass.* (in middle sense) cling to.

ingemiscō, -ere, -gemuī, groan.

ingeniōsus, -a, -um, *adj.* ingenious, clever.

ingens, -tis, *adj.* vast, mighty.

inhaereō, -ēre, -haesī, -haesum, cling to

inhospitus, -a, -um, *adj.* inhospitable, churlish.

iniciō, -ere, -iēcī, -iectum, throw over; (*pass.*) fall over.

iniustus, -a, -um, *adj.* unjust, unfair.

inmurmurō (1), murmur into, whisper into.

innectō, -ere, -nexuī, -nexum, clasp, bind.

innumerus, -a, -um, *adj.* countless, innumerable.

inquam, -is, -it, *defect. vb.,* say.

inritus, -a, -um, *adj.* vain, useless.
inrumpō, -ere, -rūpī, -ruptum, break or burst into.
insānus, -a, -um, *adj.* mad, raging.
insequor, -ī, secūtus, *dep.* follow, pursue.
insiliō, -īre, -uī, leap or spring on.
insonō, -āre, -uī, play (on a musical instrument).
instābilis, -e, *adj.* unsteady.
instructus (*part.* of **instruo**), adorned.
insurgō, -ere, -surrexī, -surrectum, arise, lift up.
intellegō, -ere, -xī, -ctum, understand.
interdum, *adv.* sometimes.
intereā, *adv.* meanwhile.
intereō, -īre, -iī, -itum, perish.
internōdium, -iī, *n.* space between joints (of leg, etc.).
interrumpō, -ere, -rūpī, -ruptum, interrupt.
interveniō, -īre, -vēnī, -ventum, come between, take place between.
intimus, -a, -um, *adj.* innermost.
intrā, *adv.* inside.
intrō (1), enter.
intus, *adv.* inside.
inūtilis, -e, *adj.* useless; ruinous.
invādō, -ere, -sī, -sum, burst into, invade; fall upon.
invehō, -ere, -vexī, -vectum, bear or carry into.
inveniō, -īre, -vēnī, -ventum, find.
invidiōsus, -a, -um, envied, coveted.
invīsus, -a, -um, *adj.* hateful.
invītō (1), encourage, induce, invite.
invītus, -a, -um, *adj.* unwilling.
invius, -a, -um, *adj.* inaccessible, pathless.
invocō (1), call upon, invoke.
ira, -ae, *f.* anger, fury.
Īris, -idis, *f.* goddess of the rainbow, messenger of Juno.
iste, -a, ud, *demonstr. pron.* that.
iter, -ineris, *n.* way, course, journey.
iterum, *adv.* again.
iubeō, -ēre, iussī, iussum, order, bid.
iūdex, -icis, *m.* judge, adjudicator.
iūdicium, -iī, *n.* decision, verdict.
iugulō (1), kill, murder.
iugum, -ī, *n.* ridge.
iunctim, *adv.* together, side by side.
iuncus, -ī, *m.* rush, reed.
iungō, -ere, -nxī, -nctum, join.
Iūnō, -ōnis, *f.* wife of Jupiter.

Iuppiter, Iovis, *m.* king of the gods.
iūrō (1), swear.
iussum, -ī, *n.* command.
iuvenca, -ae, *f.* heifer.
iuvencus, -ī, *m.* bullock, steer.
iuvenis, -is, *adj.* young; as *subst.* youth, young man.
iuventa, -ae, *f.* (time of) youth.
iūvō, -āre, iūvī, iūtum, help, assist.

labō (1), totter, shake, be weakened.
lābor, -ī, lapsus, *dep.* slip, float, drift.
labor, -ōris, *m.* toil, labour.
lac, lactis, *n.* milk, sap.
lacerō (1), tear, rend.
lacertōsus, -a, -um, *adj.* brawny, sinewy.
lacertus, -ī, *m.* arm.
lacer, -era, -erum, *adj.* torn, mangled, shattered.
lacrima, -ae, *f.* tear.
lacrimō (1), weep.
laetus, -a, -um, *adj.* glad, joyful.
laevus, -a, -um, *adj.* on the left.
lāmina, -ae, *f.* plate, sheet.
languor, -oris, *m.* weariness, sloth.
laniō (1), tear, rend.
Lāomedon, -ontis, *m.* son of Ilus and father of Priam.
Lāomedontēus, -a, -um, *adj.* of Laomedon.
lapillus, -ī, *m.* pebble.
lapis, -idis, *m.* stone.
laqueus, -ī, *m.* snare, trap.
largus, -a, -um, *adj.* copious, heavy.
lātē, *adv.* far and wide.
lateō (2), lie hid.
Lātōius, -a, -um, *adj.* of Leto or Latona; as *subst.* Apollo (Leto being the mother of Apollo and Diana).
lātus, -a, -um, *adj.* wide.
latus, -eris, *n.* side.
laurus, -ī, *f.* bay, laurel.
laus, laudis, *f.* praise, fame.
lavō, -āre, lāvī, lautum, wash.
lectus, -ī, *m.* bed.
legō, -ere, lēgī, lectum, gather, distil; read.
Lēnaeus, -ī, *m.* a name of Bacchus.
lēnīmen, -inis, *n.* solace, comfort.
lēnis, -e, *adj.* soft, gentle.

lentē, *adv.* slowly, lazily.
lentus, -a, -um, *adj.* pliant, clinging, tough.
Lesbos, -ī, *f.* Lesbos, an island in the Aegean.
lētālis, -e, *adj.* deadly.
Lēthē, -ēs, *f.* a river in the underworld; its water induced forgetfulness.
lētum, -ī, *n.* death.
levis, -e, *adj.* light; insubstantial, fleeting; trivial, slight.
leviter, *adv.* lightly, a little.
levō (1), lighten, lift; *pass.* lean on.
lex, lēgis, *f.* law; order, method.
Līber, -erī, *m.* 'the Deliverer', a name of Bacchus.
lībero (1), set free.
licet (2. *impers.*), it is allowed.
lignum, -ī, *n.* wood.
ligo, -onis, *m.* mattock.
ligō (1), bind, tie.
līmen, -inis, *n.* threshold.
lingua, -ae, *f.* tongue; speech, voice.
linquō, -ere, līquī, leave.
liquet, -ēre, līquit, *impers.* it is clear, evident.
liquidus, -a, -um, *adj.* clear, limpid; yielding.
littera, -ae, *f.* letter; inscription, epitaph.
lītus, -oris, *n.* shore.
locō (1), place, set.
locus, -ī, *m.* place (*pl.* **loci** and **loca**).
longē, *adv.* far off, far.
longus, -a, -um, *adj.* long; tedious, wearisome.
loquor, -ī, locūtus, speak, say.
Lūcifer, -erī, *m.* the morning star; the dawn.
luctus, -ūs, *m.* grief.
lūcus, -ī, *m.* grove; clump, cluster.
lūgeō, -ēre, luxī, luctum, lament, mourn.
lūgūbris, -e, *adj.* mournful; as *subst.* **lugubria, -ium,** *n. pl.* mourning garments.
lūmen, -inis, *n.* light, eye.
lūna, -ae, *f.* moon.
lupus, -ī, *m.* wolf.
lūridus, -a, -um, *adj.* wan, ghastly.
lux, lūcis, *f.* light; daylight, day.
Lyaeus, -ī, *m.* a name of Bacchus.
Lȳdus, -a, -um, *adj.* Lydian.
lymphātus, -a, -um, *adj.* maddened, distraught.
lyra, -ae, *f.* lute, lyre.

maciēs, -ēī, *f.* leanness.

maculōsus, -a, -um, *adj.* spotted.

madidus, -a, -um, *adj.* wet, dripping.

Maenades, -um, *f. pl.* Maenads, women followers of Bacchus.

maereō (2), mourn.

maestus, -a, -um, *adj.* sad, sorrowing.

magis, *compar. adv.* more.

Magnētes, -um, *m. pl.* natives of Magnesia, a district of Thessaly.

magnus, -a, -um, *adj.* great.

Maia, -ae, *f.* the mother of Mercury.

male, *adv.* ill, badly; disastrously.

malum, -ī, *n.* evil, misfortune.

mālus, -ī, *m.* mast.

malus, -a, -um, *adj.* bad, evil.

mandātum, -ī, *n.* order, charge.

mandō (1), entrust, commit; charge. **se fugae mandare,** to take to flight.

māne, *adv.* in the morning.

maneo, -ēre, mansī, mansum, await, be in store; remain.

manifestus, -a, -um, *adj.* clear, plain.

manus, -ūs, *f.* hand; handiwork, craftsmanship.

mare, -is, *n.* sea.

marīnus, -a, -um, *adj.* of the sea.

marītus, -ī, *m.* husband.

marmor, -oris, *n.* marble.

massa, -ae, *f.* lump.

māter, -tris, *f.* mother; matron.

mātūrescō, -ere, -uī, ripen.

mātūrus, -a, -um, *adj.* ripe.

mātūtīnus, -a, -um, *adj.* morning.

medius, -a, -um, *adj.* middle (of); ordinary, humble.

membrum, -ī, *n.* limb; part, piece.

meminī, *defect. vb,* remember, think of, recall.

memor, oris, *adj.* mindful.

memorō (1), tell, relate.

mens, -tis, *f.* mind, feeling, senses.

mensa, -ae, *f.* table.

mentior (4), *dep.* lie, declare falsely; counterfeit, feign.

mentum, -ī, *n.* chin.

merces, -ēdis, *f.* reward, recompense.

mergō, -ere, mersī, mersum, plunge, sink, overwhelm; in *pass.* dive.

mergus, -ī, *m.* diver.

meritus (*part.* of **mereor**) deserving; offending, guilty.

merum, -ī, *n.* unmixed wine; wine.

messis, -is, *f.* harvest, crop.
Mēthymnaeus, -a, -um, *adj.* of Methymna, a town in Lesbos.
metus, -ūs, *m.* fear.
micō (1), flash, gleam.
Midas, -ae, *m.* (*acc.* **Midan**), king of Phrygia.
mīles, -itis, *m.* soldier.
mīlitia, -ae, *f.* military service; (*collective*) soldiery.
minax, -ācis, *adj.* threatening.
minister, -trī, *m.* servant.
ministerium, -iī, *n.* employment, labour.
mīrāculum, -ī, *n.* marvel, wonder.
mīrus, -a, -um, *adj.* strange, marvellous.
misceō, -ēre, -uī, mixtum, mix; throw into confusion, trouble.
miser, -era, -erum, *adj.* wretched.
miserābilis, -e, *adj.* pitiful, wretched.
miserandus (*gerundive* of **miseror**), pitiable, unfortunate.
misereor (2) *dep.* pity.
miseror (1) *dep.* pity.
mītis, -e, *adj.* mild, merciful.
mitto, -ere, mīsī, missum, send, dismiss; hurl, shoot.
modo, *adv.* only, but; lately, recently; **modo . . . modo,** now . . . now.
modulor (1), *dep.* tune, play.
modus, -ī, *m.* moderation.
moenia, -ium, *n. pl.* walls; ramparts, bulwarks.
mōles, -is, *f.* pile, weight, mass; pier, mole.
mōlior (4), labour at, toil at; raise, construct.
molliō (4), soften, soothe, appease.
mollis, -e, *adj.* soft, gentle.
molliter, *adv.* softly.
mōmentum, -ī, *n.* decisive factor.
mons, -tis, *m.* mountain.
monstrum, -ī, *n.* monster, prodigy, portent.
montānus, -a, -um, *adj.* mountain, upland.
mora, -ae, *f.* delay.
moror (1), delay, linger.
Morpheus, -eī and **-eōs** (*acc.* Morphea), god of dreams, son of Somnus.
mors, -tis, *f.* death.
mortālis, -e, mortal, human.
mōtō (1), move about.
mōtus, -ūs, *m.* movement.
moveō, -ēre, mōvī, mōtum, move, shake, stir; cause, excite; influence, affect; take up, wield.
mulceō, -ēre, mulsī, mulsum, soothe, lull.
multō, *adv.* much, by far.

multum, *adv.* very.
multus, -a, -um, *adj.* much, many.
mundus, -ī, *m.* world.
mūniō (4), fortify, make secure.
mūnus, -eris, *n.* gift; office, use, purpose.
mūrex, -icis, *m.* purple.
murmur, -uris, *n.* murmur, moaning.
murmurō (1), murmur.
mūrus, -ī, *m.* wall.
mūtō (1), change.
mūtus, -a, -um, *adj.* dumb, voiceless.
myrteus, -a, -um, *adj.* of myrtle.

nāis, -idis, *f.* water-nymph, Naiad.
nam, namque, *conj.* for.
narrō (1), tell, relate.
natō (1), swim, float.
nātus (*part.* of **nascor**), born, created; as *subst. m.* or *f.,* son, daughter.
naufragus, -a, -um, *adj.* shipwrecked; as *subst.* a shipwrecked person.
nāvāle, -is, *n.* dock.
nāvigium, -iī, *n.* ship, vessel.
nāvita, -ae, *m.* sailor.
nebula, -ae, *f.* cloud, mist.
nec, neque, *conj.* and not, nor, neither.
nefas, *indeclin. noun,* sin, evil deed.
negō (1), deny, refuse.
Nephelēis, -idis, *f.* daughter of Nephele, i.e. Helle.
nepos, -ōtis, *m.* grandson, descendant.
nequeō, -īre, -iī, -itum, be unable.
nēquīquam, *adv.* in vain.
Nēreus, -ī, *m.* a sea god.
Nērēis, -idos, *f.* a sea nymph, daughter of Nereus.
nervus, -ī, *m.* string.
nesciō (4), be ignorant of; **nescioquid,** something (cf. French 'je ne sais quoi').
neu, nēve, *conj.* and not, and lest.
(nex), necis, *f.* death.
nīdus, -ī, *m.* nest.
niger, -gra, grum, *adj.* black.
nihil, nīl, *indecl.* noun, nothing.
nimbōsus, -a, -um, *adj.* rainy, stormy.
nimbus, -ī, *m.* storm-cloud, storm.
nimium, *adv.* too much.
nisi, *conj.* unless, if not.

nitens, -entis (*part.* of **niteō**), shining, bright.
niteō (2), shine.
nitidus, -a, -um, *adj.* brilliant; polished, elegant, refined.
nitor, -ōris, *m.* brightness, sheen, lustre.
nītor, -ī, nīsus (nīxus), *dep.* struggle, strive.
nō (1), swim.
noceō (2), hurt, harm, prove ruin of.
nōlō, nolle, nōluī, be unwilling.
nōmen, -inis, *n.* name, inscription; fame, renown.
nōminō (1), name, call.
nondum, *adv.* not yet.
noscō, -ere, nōvī, nōtum, know, recognise.
nota, -ae, *f.* mark, sign (l. 466, wave).
notō (1), mark, distinguish.
noviens, *adv.* nine times.
novissimus, -a, -um, *adj.* last, latest.
novitas, -tātis, *f.* novelty; strangeness.
novō (1), alter.
novus, -a, -um, *adj.* new, fresh; strange, unheard of.
nox, -ctis, *f.* night.
nūbes, -is, *f.* cloud.
nūbila, -ōrum, *n. pl.* clouds.
nūbilis, -e, *adj.* ripe for marriage.
nūbilus, -a, -um, *adj.* cloud-bringing.
nūdus, -a, -um, *adj.* naked.
nullus, -a, -um, *adj.* no, none.
nūmen, -inis, *n.* assent; divine power, godhead, god.
numerus, -ī, *m.* number; band, body.
numquam, *adv.* never.
nunc, *adv.* now.
nuntia, -ae, *f.* a (woman) messenger.
nuntius, -iī, *m.* messenger.
nūper, *adv.* recently, lately.
nurus, -ūs, *f.* (married) woman.
nūtō (1), nod.
Nympha, -ae (or **-e, -es**), *f.* a Nymph.

ob, *prep.* + *acc.* on account of.
obeō, -īre, -iī, -itum, come over, overspread.
oblectāmen, -inis, *n.* delight, consolation.
oblitus (*part.* of **oblinō**), smeared.
obnoxius, -a, -um, subject to, exposed to.
oborior, -īrī, -ortus, rise up, well up.
obruō, -ere, -ruī, -rutum, cover up, bury, overwhelm.

obscūrus, -a, -um, *adj.* hidden, shrouded.
obsessus (*part.* of **obsideō**), beset, overgrown.
obsitus (*part.* of **obserō**), filled, covered.
obstō, -āre, -stitī, stand in way of; oppose, hinder.
obstrepō, -ere, -uī, -itum, resound against, drown (of sound).
obstrūsus (*part.* of **obtrūdō**), edged, bordered.
obsum, -esse, -fuī, hinder, ruin, be fatal.
obvertō, -ere, -ī, sum, turn towards.
obvius, -a, -um, *adj.* meeting, to meet, facing; **obvius undis,** upstream.
occidō, -ere, -cidī, -cāsum, perish, die.
occupō (1), take, seize; take first.
oculus, -ī, *m.* eye.
ōdī, *defect. vb,* hate, curse.
Oetaeus, -a, -um, *adj.* of Oeta, a mountain near Trachis; **rex Oetaeus,**
     Ceyx.
ōlim, *adv.* formerly; sometimes.
ōmen, -inis, *n.* omen.
omnis, -e, *adj.* all.
Onētor, -oris, *m.* Peleus' herdsman.
opācus, -a, -um, *adj.* shady, dark.
operiō, -īre, -uī, -ertum, cover.
oppugnō (1), attack, assault.
(ops), opis, *f.* aid, relief; in *pl.* wealth, expense.
optō (1), wish for, desire; choose.
opus, -eris, *n.* work, task.
ōra, -ae, *f.* shore.
orbis, -is, *m.* circle, orb; orbit.
orbus, -a, -um, *adj.* bereaved.
ordo, -inis, *m.* order, line, row; **ordine,** successively.
orgia, -ōrum, *n. pl.* Bacchic rites, mysteries.
orīgo, -inis, *f.* birth, origin; ancestor.
orior, -īrī, ortus, *dep.* rise.
ornō (1), decorate, adorn.
ōrō (1), pray, beg.
Orpheus, -eī (*acc.* **Orphea**), a legendary bard.
Orphēus, -a, -um, *adj.* of Orpheus.
ortus, -ūs, *m.* rising, source.
os, ossis, *n.* bone.
ōs, ōris, *n.* face, mouth, face, lips; bill, beak; gaze, look.
osculum, -ī, *n.* kiss.
ostendō, -ere, -dī, -sum, show, point to.

paciscor, -ī, pactus, *dep.* bargain, bargain for.
Pactōlos, -ī, *m.* (*acc.* **Pactolon**), a river in Lydia.

pactum, -ī, *n.* agreement.

palla, -ae, *f.* long robe.

pallescō, -ere, -uī, grow pale, sallow.

pallor, -ōris, *m.* paleness.

palma, -ae, *f.* palm, hand.

palus, -ūdis, *f.* marsh.

palustris, -e, *adj.* of a marsh.

Pān, -os (*acc.* **Pāna**), *m.* the god of woods and shepherds.

pandō, -ere, -ī, passum, spread out.

Panomphaeus, -ī, *m.* 'author of oracles', an epithet of Jupiter.

papāver, -eris, *n.* poppy.

parātus (*part.* of **parō**), prepared, ready.

parens, -ntis, *c.* parent.

pariō, -ere, peperī, partum, bear, bring forth.

pariter, *adv.* equally, alike, at the same time.

Parnāsis, -idis, *adj.* of Parnassus.

Parnāsus, -ī, *f.* a mountain on Phocis, sacred to Apollo and the Muses.

parō (1), prepare, make ready; strive.

pars, -tis, *f.* part, side, portion, share; **pars . . . pars,** some . . . others.

parvus, -a, -um, *adj.* small; **parva voce,** in a low voice.

passim, *adv.* everywhere, on all sides.

passus (*part.* of **pandō**), loose, dishevelled.

pateō (2), be open, be accessible.

pater, -tris, *m.* father.

paternus, -a, -um, *adj.* of a father.

patior, -ī, passus, *dep.* bear, allow, suffer.

patria, -ae, *f.* native land.

patrius, -a, -um, *adj.* of a father.

patulus, -a, -um, *adj.* open, wide.

paucus, -a, -um, *adj.* few.

paulum, *adv.* a little.

paveō, -ēre, pāvī, fear, tremble, be terrified.

peccō (1), sin.

pectus, -oris, *n.* breast, heart.

pecus, -udis, *f.* beast, animal.

pecus, -oris, *n.* cattle, herd, flock.

pelagus, -ī, *n.* sea.

Pēleus, -eī and **-eos** (*acc.* **Pēlea**), *m.* father of Achilles.

pendeō, -ēre, pependī, hover, hang; sag; float (746).

penetrāle, -is, *n.* inmost place, sanctuary.

penna, -ae, *f.* wing.

per, *prep.* + *acc.* through, during, by means of, over.

peragō, -ere, -ēgī, -actum, perform, fulfil.

percipiō, -ere, -cēpī, -ceptum, gather, absorb, take in.
percutiō, -ere, -cussī, -cussum, strike, smite, beat.
perdō, -ere, -didī, -ditum, destroy, lose, waste.
peregrīnus, -a, -um, *adj.* foreign.
pereō, -īre, -iī, perish.
pererrō (1), wander among.
perfidia, -ae, *f.* treachery, faithlessness.
perīculum (perīclum), -ī, *n.* danger.
perimō, -ere, -ēmī, -emptum, destroy.
periūrium, -iī, *n.* false oath, perjury.
periūrus, -a, -um, *adj.* false, forsworn.
perōsus (*part.* of **perōdī**), loathing, detesting.
perpetuus, -a, -um, *adj.* continuous, unbroken.
perstō, -āre, -stitī, -stitum, continue, persist.
perterreō (2), frighten.
perveniō, -īre, -vēnī, -ventum, come to, reach.
pēs, pedis, *m.* foot.
petō, -ere, -īvī (-iī) -ītum, seek, ask; make for; attack.
Philammōn, -ōnis, *m.* son of Chione by Apollo.
Phlegyae, -ārum, *m. pl.* a Thessalian tribe.
Phobētōr, -oris, *m.* a name of Icelos.
Phōcēus, -a, -um, *adj.* Phocian.
Phōcus, -ī, *m.* son of Aeacus and Psamathe.
Phoebus, -ī, *m.* a name of Apollo; the sun.
Phorbas, -antis, *m.* a plunderer of Apollo's sanctuary at Delphi.
Phryges, -um, *m. pl.* Phrygians.
Phrygia, -ae, *f.* a district of Asia Minor.
Phrygius, -a, -um, *adj.* Phrygian.
piceus, -a, -um, *adj.* pitchy, pitch black.
piget (2), *impers.* it grieves; one repents.
pignus, -oris, *n.* pledge, security; child, offspring.
Pindus, -ī, *m.* a mountain in Thessaly.
pinguis, -e, *adj.* fat; lazy; dull, stupid.
pīnus, -ūs and -ī, *f.* pine; ship.
pius, -a, -um, *adj.* devout, loyal, dutiful, loving.
placeō (2), please, satisfy, seem good.
placidus, -a, -um, *adj.* gentle, quiet, calm.
plācō (1), calm.
plaga, -ae, *f.* region, district.
plangō, -ere, -nxī, -nctum, strike, beat the breast, etc.; in *pass.* beat oneself, mourn.
plangor, -ōris, *m.* beating (of the breast, etc.), lamentation.
plausus, -ūs, *m.* clapping of hands.
plebs, -is, *f.* common people.

plectrum, -ī, *n.* quill (for plucking the lyre).
plēnus, -a, -um, *adj.* full, complete.
plūma, -ae, *f.* feather, plumage.
plūmeus, -a, -um, *adj.* made of feathers, down.
poena, -ae, *f.* punishment, penalty.
pollex, -icis, *m.* thumb.
polliceor (2), *dep.* promise.
pollicitum, -ī, *n.* promise.
pōmum, -ī, *n.* fruit.
pondus, -eris, *n.* weight.
pōnō, -ere, posuī, positum, put, place, set; lay aside, shed.
pontus, -ī, *m.* sea.
populāris, -e, *adj.* native.
populus, -ī, *m.* people, nation, crowd.
porrectus, *part.* of **porrigō.**
porrigō, -ere, -rexī, -rectum, stretch out, extend.
portus, -ūs, *m.* harbour.
poscō, -ere, poposcī, demand, ask the surrender of.
possum, posse, potuī, can, be able.
postis, -is, *m.* doorpost, door.
potens, -ntis, *adj.* powerful.
potior (4), *dep.* obtain; attain, reach.
prae, *prep.* + *abl.* before, in comparison with.
praebeō (2), give, afford.
praecēdō, -ere, -cessī, -cessu, go before, lead the way.
praeceps, -cipitis, *adj.* headlong.
praecipitō (1), drive down, rush down, fall headlong.
praecordia, -ōrum, *n. pl.* heart.
praeda, -ae, *f.* booty, prey.
praedēlassō (1), weary or tire out beforehand.
praeferō, -ferre, -tulī, -lātum, rank above, prefer.
praeripiō, -ere, -ripuī, reptum, steal beforehand.
praesāgus, -a, -um, *adj.* prophetic, having previous knowledge of.
praesens, -ntis, *adj.* present, in person.
praestans, -ntis, *adj.* distinguished, pre-eminent.
praestō, -āre, -stitī, -stitum, fulfil; make secure, safe.
praesūtus (*part.* of **praesuō**), sown over, tipped.
praetendō, -ere, -dī, -tum, stretch forth, hold before.
praeter, *prep.* + *acc.* besides, except.
praetereō, -īre, -iī, -itum, pass over, pass by.
praevius, -a, -um, leading the way.
precor (1), pray.
premō, -ere, pressī, pressum, press, push down; cover, overlay.
pretium, -iī, *n.* reward, wages.

prex, precis, *f.* prayer, entreaty.
Priamus, -ī, *m.* king of Troy.
prīmō, *adv.* at first.
prīmum, *adv.* first; **ut prīmum,** as soon as.
prīmus, -a, -um, *adj.* first, earliest.
prior, -ius *adj.* former.
prius, *adv.* sooner, before.
priusquam, *conj.* before.
prō, *prep.* + *abl.* before, for.
prō, *interj.* O! alas! (*foll.* by *nom.* or *acc.*).
probō (1), make acceptable.
procella, -ae, *f.* tempest.
procul, *adv.* far.
prōcurrō, -ere, cucurrī, jut or run out.
procus, -ī, *m.* wooer, suitor.
prōdigium, -iī, *n.* marvel, portent.
prōdō, -ere, -didī, -ditum, bring forward, publish, betray.
profānus, -a, -um, *adj.* impious.
profor (1), *dep.* say, speak.
profugus, -a, -um, *adj.* exiled.
profundō, -ere, -fūdī, -fūsum, shed, pour forth.
profundum, -ī, *n.* deep.
prōgeniēs, -ēī, *f.* offspring, descendant.
prōgenitor, -ōris, *m.* ancestor, grandfather.
prohibeō (2), prevent.
prōles, -is, *f.* offspring.
prōmissum, -ī, *n.* promise.
prōmittō, -ere, -mīsī, -missum, promise.
prōnus, -a, -um, *adj.* headfirst; sinking.
propāgo, inis, *f.* offspring, child.
prope, *prep.* + *acc.* near; *adv.* near.
properō (1), hasten.
propinquus, -a, -um, *adj.* near.
prōpōnō, -ere, -posuī, -positum, intend.
prōsiliō, -īre, -uī, spring or start forward.
prōspiciō, -ere, -spexī, -spectum, look out on, overlook.
prōsum, prōdesse, prōfuī, be profitable.
prōtendō, -ere, -ī, -tum or **-sum,** stretch or hold out.
prōtinus, *adv.* straightway.
proximus, -a, -um, *adj.* nearest, next, neighbouring.
Psamathē, -ēs, *f.* a sea-nymph.
pudor, -ōris, *m.* shame, disgrace, deformity.
pugnō (1), fight, strive.
pulcher, -chra, -chrum, *adj.* beautiful, fair.

pullus, -a, -um, *adj.* dark-coloured; as *subst.* **pullum, -ī,** *n.* black robe of mourning.
pulsō (1), beat, batter.
puppis, -is, *f.* stern; ship.
purpureus, -a, -um, *adj.* purple.
purgāmen, -inis, *n.* purification, expiation.
pŭrus, -a, -um, *adj.* pure, clear.
putō (1), think, suppose.

quā, *adv.* where; **si qua,** if anywhere.
quaerō, -ere, quaesīvī, quaesītum, ask, seek.
quālis, -e, *rel adj.* such as; *interrog. adj.* of what kind?
quāliscumque, *rel. adj.* of whatever kind.
quam, *adv.* how; than.
quamquam, *conj.* although.
quamvīs, *conj.* although.
quantus, -a, -um, *adj.* how great, as great as; **in quantum,** as far as.
quasi, *adv.* as if, as it were, just like.
quater, *adv.* four times.
quercus, -ūs, *f.* oak; oak-leaves.
querella, -ae, *f.* complaint.
queror, -ī, questus, *dep.* complain.
quia, *conj.* because.
quīcumque, *indef. pron.* whoever, whatever.
quid, *interrog. adv.* why?
quidem, *adv.* indeed.
quiēs, -ētis, *f.* rest, sleep, stillness.
quiescō, -ere, quiēvī, quiētum, rest.
quippe, *adv.* and *conj.* for indeed, since in fact.
quis, quid, *indef. pron.* anyone, anything (after **si, ne**).
quis, quid, *interrog. pron.* who? what?
quisquam, quaequam, quicquam, *indef. pron.* any.
quisque, quaeque, quidque, *pron.* each.
quisquis, quodquod, *indef. pron.* whoever, whatever.
quō, *adv.* whither, to which.
quodsī, *conj.* but if.
quoniam, *conj.* because.
quoque, *conj.* also.
quot, *indeclin. adj.* how many, as many as.
quotiens, *adv.* as often as.

rabiēs, -ēī, *f.* rage.
radiō (1), flash, gleam.

radius, -iī, *m.* ray.
rādix, -īcis, *f.* root.
rāmus, -ī, *m.* branch.
rapiō, -ere, uī, -ptum, seize, carry off, snatch up; hurry.
raptum, -ī, *n.* prey, spoil, plunder.
rārus, -a, -um, *adj.* rare (*adv.* **rārō,** seldom).
rāstrum, -ī, *n.* rake (*irreg. pl.* **rastrī**).
ratis, -is, *f.* ship, craft.
raucus, -a, -um, *adj.* hoarse, deep-sounding, booming.
recēdō, -ere, -cessī, -cessum, pass away, depart, retire, recede.
recens, -ntis, *adj.* fresh, newly-grown.
recessus, -ūs, *m.* retreat, recess.
recipiō, -ere, -cēpī, -ceptum, recover, take, receive.
recognoscō, -ere, -gnōvī, -gnitum, recall, recognise.
recondō, -ere, -didī, -ditum, hide or bury again.
rector, -ōris, *m.* ruler, governor; steersman.
recurrō, -ere, currī, run or hurry back.
recursus, -ūs, *m.* return.
recurvus, -a, -um, *adj.* curved.
reddō, -ere, -didī, -ditum, restore, return; emit, let out.
redeō, -īre, -iī, -itum, return.
reditus, -ūs, *m.* return.
redūcō, -ere, -xī, -ctum, bring back, draw back.
referō, -ferre, rettulī, relātum, tell, report, relate; repeat.
reformō (1), shape again.
refundō, -ere, -fūdī, -fūsum, pour, pour back.
regerō, -ere, -gessī, -gestum, carry back, put back.
regimen, -inis, *n.* rudder.
rēgīna, -ae, *f.* queen.
rēgius, -a, -um, *adj.* of a king, royal.
regnō (1), rule, reign.
regnum, -ī, *n.* realm.
regō, -ere, -xī, -ctum, rule, govern.
relābor, -ī, -lapsus, slip back.
relegō, -ere, -lēgī, -lectum, regain.
relevō (1), relieve.
relinquō, -ere, -līquī, -lictum, leave, forsake.
relūceō, -ēre, -luxī, gleam, shine, glow.
remeō (1), return.
reminiscōr, -ī, *dep.* recall to mind, recollect.
remittō, -ere, -mīsī, -missum, send back; allow, permit.
remoror (1), *dep.* delay, clog.
removeō, -ēre, -mōvī, -mōtum, withdraw; (*reflex.* or in *pass.*) retire, hold aloof from.

rēmus, -ī, *m.* oar.
renovō (1), renew.
reor, -ērī, ratus, *dep.* think.
reparō (1), refresh, revive.
repellō, -ere, reppulī, repulsum, drive back, foil, repel.
repetō, -ere, -iī, -ītum, seek again.
repugnō (1), resist.
rēs, -ēī, *f.* thing, matter, affair.
resecō (1), cut off.
resolvō, -ere, -vī, -ūtum, loosen, break.
rēspiciō, -ere, -spexī, -spectum, look back (at).
rēspondeō, -ēre, -dī, -sum, answer, echo.
rēstagnō (1), overflow.
rēstituō, -ere, -uī, -ūtum, restore (to a former condition).
rēte, -is, *n.* net.
retemptō (1), try again.
reticeō (2), keep silence, conceal.
retināculum, -ī, *n.* cable, hawser.
retineō (2), keep back, hold back, retain.
retorqueō, -ēre, -torsī, -tortum, bend or turn back.
revellō, -ere, -vellī, -volsum (-vulsum), tear away, wrench off.
revertor, -ī, versus, return.
revinciō, -īre, -vinxī, -vinctum, bind or tie behind.
revocō (1), recall.
rex, rēgis, *m.* king.
rictus, -ūs, *m.* gaping jaws.
rigeō (2), be stiff, hard; stand stiffly.
rigidus, -a, -um, *adj.* stiff, hard, unbending, rocky.
rigō (1), moisten, bedew.
rīma, -ae, *f.* chink, seam.
rīpa, -ae, *f.* bank.
rīvus, -ī, *m.* stream; channel, bed.
rōbur, -oris, *n.* oak, timber.
Roeteus, -a, -um, *adj.* of Roeteum, a town and promontory in the Troad.
rogō (1), ask.
rogus, -ī, *m.* funeral pyre.
rōs, rōris, *m.* dew; drop.
rostrum, -ī, *n.* beak.
ruber, -ra, -rum, *adj.* red.
rubescō, -ere, rubuī, grow red.
rudens, -ntis, *n.* rope, line; in *pl.* rigging.
rūmor, -ōris, *m.* report.
rumpō, -ere, rūpī, ruptum, break, burst.

ruō, -ere, ruī, rutum, rush.
ruricola, -ae, *adj.* rustic.
rursus, *adv.* again.
rūs, rūris, *n.* country.
rutilus, -a, -um, *adj.* red-gleaming, fiery-red.

sacer, -cra, -crum, *adj.* holy, sacred.
sacra, -ōrum, *n. pl.* holy rites, mysteries.
sacrilegus, -a, -um, *adj.* violating holy things; impious, wicked.
sacrō (1), dedicate, consecrate.
saepe, *adv.* often.
saeviō (4), rage.
sagax, -ācis, *adj.* keen of sense, vigilant.
sagitta, -ae, *f.* arrow.
salictum, -ī, *n.* plantation or thicket of willows.
saltem, *adv.* at least.
saltus, -ūs, *m.* leap.
sanctus, -a, -um, *adj.* holy, sacred.
sanguis, -inis, *m.* blood.
sarculum, -ī, *n.* hoe.
Sardēs, -ium, *f. pl.* Sardis, the capital of Lydia.
satis, *adv.* enough; quite; with *neg.* not very.
saturātus (*part.* of **saturō**), steeped, deep-dyed.
satus (*part.* of **serō**), sprung from, begotten by.
Satyrī, -ōrum, *m. pl.* the Satyrs, goat-footed followers of Bacchus.
saucius, -a, -um, *adj.* wounded.
saxum, -ī, *n.* stone, rock.
scelerātus, -a, -um, *adj.* wicked, guilty.
scelus, -eris, *n.* crime.
sceptrum, -ī, *n.* sceptre.
scindō, -ere, scīdī, scissum, tear, rend.
scītor (1), inquire.
scrobis, -is, *m.* pit, hole.
sēcēdō, -ere, -cessī, -cessum, go apart, withdraw.
secō, -āre, secuī, sectum, cut, furrow.
sēcrētus (*part.* of **sēcernō**), remote.
sēcūrus, -a, -um, *adj.* free of care, unconcerned.
secus, *adv.* otherwise; *comp.* **setius; haud setius quam,** just as.
sēdes, -is, *f.* seat, place, abode; base, foundation.
semel, *adv.* once.
sēmen, -inis, *n.* seed, grain.
semper, *adv.* always.
senex, senis, *m.* old; as *subst.* old man; *comp.* **senior,** elder.
sensus, -ūs, *m.* feeling, sense.

sententia, -ae, *f.* opinion; award, verdict; resolve.
sentiō, -īre, sensī, sensum, feel, perceive, experience.
sepulchrum, -ī, *n.* tomb.
sequor, -ī, secūtus, *dep.* follow.
sermo, -ōnis, *m.* talk.
serpens, -tis, *c.* snake.
servō (1), preserve, keep.
setius, see **secus.**
seu, *conj.* whether, or.
sī, *conj.* if; **sī quis,** if any one, whoever; **sī quando,** whenever.
sī quidem, if indeed, since.
sīc, *adv.* so, thus.
siccō (1), dry.
sīdereus, -a, -um, *adj.* starry, star-born.
Sīgēus, -a, -um, *adj.* of Sigeum, a town and promontory in the Troad.
signō (1), mark.
signum, -ī, *n.* sign, signal.
silentium, -iī, *n.* silence.
Sīlēnus, -ī, *m.* an old Satyr, foster-father of Bacchus.
silex, -icis, *m.* flint.
silva, -ae, *f.* wood, forest.
similis, -e, *adj.* like.
simul, *adv.* together, at the same time; *conj.* as soon as.
simulācrum, -ī, *n.* image, representation.
simulātor, -ōris, *m.* imitator, feigner.
simulō (1), counterfeit, imitate.
sine, *prep.* + *abl.* without.
singulī, -ae, -a, *adj.* one by one, one after the other.
singultus, -ūs, *m.* sobbing.
sinō, -ere, sīvī, situm, allow, permit.
sinuō (1), bend, swell, curve.
sinus, -ūs, *m.* bay.
sitis, -is, *f.* thirst.
sīve, *conj.* whether, or.
socer, -erī, *m.* father-in-law.
sociō (1), join, unite; accompany.
socius, -iī, *m.* comrade, partner.
sōl, sōlis, *m.* sun.
sōlācium, -iī, *n.* consolation, comfort.
soleō, -ēre, solitus, *semi-dep.* be accustomed.
solidus, -a, -um, *adj.* solid, firm.
solitus (*part.* of **soleō**), accustomed.
sollerter, *adv.* skilfully. *Compar.* **sollertius.**
sollicitō (1), touch, stir, strike, ply.

sollicitus, -, a-um, *adj.* restless, wakeful.

sōlor (1), *dep.* comfort.

sōlum, *adv.* only.

solum, -i, *n.* soil, ground.

sōlus, -a, -um, *adj.* alone.

solvō, -ere, -vī, -ūtum, loosen, relax; do away, annul; break up; pay, fulfil, discharge.

somnium, -iī, *n.* dream, vision.

somnus, -ī, *m.* sleep; *personified,* Somnus, the god of sleep.

sonō, -āre, -uī, -itum, sound, resound, roar; cry, shout; creak.

sons, sontis, *adj.* guilty.

sonus, -ī, *m.* sound, noise.

sōpiō (4), lull to sleep.

sopor, -ōris, *m.* heavy sleep, slumber.

sopōrifer, -fera, -ferum, *adj.* sleep-bringing or inducing.

sors, sortis, *f.* lot; in *pl.* oracle.

sortior (4), *dep.* draw by lot, obtain, receive.

sōspes, -itis, *adj.* safe.

spargō, -ere, sparsī, sparsum, scatter, sprinkle.

spatior (1), *dep.* walk, stroll.

spatiōsus, -a, -um, *adj.* long.

spatium, -iī, *n.* space, distance.

speciēs, -ēī, *f.* sight, shape, appearance.

speciōsus, -a, -um, *adj.* showy, brilliant, (deceptively) alluring.

spectō (1), see, watch, regard.

specus, -ūs, *m.* cave, grotto.

spēlunca, -ae, *f.* cave, cavern.

spēs, -ēī, *f.* hope.

spīculum, -ī, *n.* sting.

spīrō (1), blow.

spissus, -a, -um, *adj.* thick, clotted.

splendidus, -a, -um, *adj.* shining, glistening.

spolia, -ōrum, *n. pl.* spoils.

spoliō (1), strip, deprive.

sponte, *adv.* of one's own accord.

spūma, -ae, *f.* spume, saliva, foam.

spūmiger, -era, -erum, *adj.* foaming.

stāmen, -inis, *n.* string.

status, -ūs, *m.* position, situation; attitude, pose.

stella, -ae, *f.* star.

sternō, -ere, strāvī, strātum, spread, smooth; strew, scatter; strike down, lay low.

stillō (1), drop, drip.

stirps, stirpis, *f.* stock.

stō, stāre, stetī, statum, stand.
stolidus, -a, -um, *adj.* dull, stupid, senseless.
strātum, -ī, *n.* coverlet, pillow; couch, bed.
strepitō (1), make a noise, din, crashing.
strepitus, -ūs, *m.* noise, din; (of wings) flapping, whirring.
strīdor, -ōris, *m.* creaking.
stringō, -ere, -nxī, -ctum, touch lightly, skim; sting.
struō, -ere, -xī, -ctum, build, pile up.
stupeō (2), be aghast.
Stygius, -a, -um, *adj.* of the Styx, a river of the underworld.
sub, *prep.* + *abl.* under; + *acc.* under, up to, beneath; (of time) towards.
subdō, -ere, -didī, -ditum, put under.
subdūcō, -ere, -xī, -ctum, draw up, stow, ship.
subedō, -ere, ēdī, eat or wear away from below.
subeō, -īre, -iī, -itum, go under, come up, enter; come to mind.
subigō, -ere, -ēgī, -actum, turn up, plough; subdue, conquer.
subitus, -a, -um. *adj.* sudden; newly made or appearing.
sublīmis, -e, *adj.* on high.
submittō, -ere, -mīsī, -missum, lower, place below.
submoveō, -ēre, -mōvī, -mōtum, remove, withdraw.
subnectō, -ere, -nexuī, -nexum, bind underneath, furl, reef in.
substrictus (*part.* of **substringō**), contracted, narrow, slender.
subsum, -esse, be under, be near.
subvolō (1), fly up.
succēdō, -ere, -cessī, -cessum, go under, come up on, take the place of, succeed to.
sūdor, -ōris, *m.* sweat, toil.
suffūsus (*part.* of **suffundō**), suffused, filled.
summus, -a, -um, *superl. adj.* highest, greatest, top of.
sūmō, -ere, -mpsī, -mptum, take, receive, put on.
super, *prep.* + *acc.* above, upon, over.
superbiō (4), be proud, take pride in.
superī, -ōrum, *m. pl.* those on high, the gods.
superō (1), conquer.
superstes, -stitis, *adj.* standing over.
supersum, -esse, -fuī, be left, remain, survive.
supplex, -icis, *adj.* suppliant, asking pardon.
supprimō, -ere, pressī, -pressum, cut short, stop.
suprēmus, -a, -um, *superl. adj.* last.
sūra, -ae, *f.* ankle.
surgō, -ere, surrexī, surrectum, rise.
susceptum, -ī, *n.* undertaking.
suspiciō, -ere, -spexī, -spectum, look up at.
sustineō (2), hold up, hold; *with infin.* dare, bear to.

tabula, -ae, *f.* board, plank.
taceō (2), be silent, quiet.
tacitus, -a, -um, *adj.* silent.
tactus, -ūs, *m.* touch.
tālis, -e, *adj.* such.
tam, *adv.* so.
tamen, *conj.* nevertheless, yet.
tamquam, *adv.* as if, just as.
tandem, *adv.* at last.
tangō, -ere, tetigī, tactum, touch; move, affect, influence.
tantō, *adv.* by so much, so much.
tantum, *adv.* only.
tantus, -a, -um, *adj.* so great.
tardus, -a, -um, *adj.* slow, lingering, slothful.
Tartarus, -ī, *m.* (*pl.* **Tartara**), the lowest depth of the underworld.
taurus, -ī, *m.* bull.
tectum, -ī, *n.* roof, dwelling.
tegmen, -inis, *n.* covering.
tegō, -ere, texī, tectum, cover, shroud.
Telamōn, -ōnis, *m.* son of Aeacus.
tellus, -ūris, *f.* earth, ground.
tēlum, -ī, *n.* weapon, spear, sword.
temerārius, -a, -um, *adj.* rash, reckless.
tēmo, -ōnis, *m.* beam of a wagon; chariot.
templum, -ī, *n.* temple.
tempora, -um, *n. pl.* brows, temples.
temptō (1), try, test.
tempus, -oris, *n.* time.
tenax, -ācis, *adj.* holding fast, secure.
tendō, -ere, tetendī, tensum, stretch, stretch out.
tenebrae, -ārum, *f. pl.* darkness.
teneō, -ēre, -uī, -ntum, hold, have, occupy; maintain; check restrain; trap, imprison; reach.
tener, -era, -erum, *adj.* tender, young.
tenuis, -e, *adj.* thin.
tepidus, -a, -um, *adj.* lukewarm.
ter, *adv.* three times, thrice.
teres, -etis, *adj.* smooth, rounded, shapely, slender.
terra, -ae, *f.* earth, land.
terreō (2), alarm, frighten.
tertius, -a, -um, *adj.* third.
Tēthys, -yos, *f.* a sea-goddess, wife of Oceanus.
textum, -ī, *n.* fabric, hull.
thalamus, -ī, *m.* bridal bed; marriage.

Thaumantis, -idos, *f.* the daughter of Thaumas, i.e. Iris.
theātrum, -ĭ, *n.* theatre.
Thetis, -idis, *f.* a sea-nymph, wife of Peleus.
Thisbaeus, -a, -um, *adj.* of Thisbe, a Boeotian town famed for its doves.
Thrācius (Thrēicius), -a, -um, *adj.* Thracian.
thyrsus, -ĭ, *m.* bacchic wand, thyrsus.
tiāra, -ae, *f.* turban, Oriental head-dress.
tībia, -ae, *f.* flute, pipe.
tīgris, -idis, *f.* tigress.
timeō (2), fear.
timidus, -a, -um, *adj.* fearful, timid.
Timōlus, -ĭ, *m.* a mountain in Lydia; the mountain-god Timolus.
timor, -ōris, *m.* fear.
tingō, -ere, nxĭ, -nctum, tinge, dye; dip, launch.
Tītān, -ānis, *m.* the sun-god.
titubō (1), totter, reel.
titulus, -ĭ, *m.* an inscription recording exploits, etc.; title; glory.
Tmōlus, see Timolus.
tolerō (1), endure.
tollō, -ere, sustulī, sublātum, raise, lift, sustain; take on board, carry; take away.
Tonans, -antis, *m.* the Thunderer, epithet of Jupiter.
tondeō, -ēre, totondī, tonsum, shear.
tonitrus, -ūs, *m.* thunder.
torqueō, -ēre, -sī, -tum, twist, hurl; torture, mock.
torus, -ĭ, *m.* couch.
tostus (*part.* of **torreō**), roasted, parched, baked.
tot, *indeclin. adj.* so many.
totidem, *indeclin. adj.* so many; the same number.
tōtus, -a, -um, *adj.* the whole.
trabs, trabis, *f.* beam; tree, trunk.
Trāchīs, -īnis, *f.* a Thessalian city, Ceyx' kingdom.
Trāchīnius, -a, -um, *adj.* of Trachis; as *subst.* Ceyx.
trādō, -ere, -didī, -ditum, hand over, impart.
trahō, -ere, -xī, -ctum, draw, drag; lead, bring; draw out; swallow; get, catch.
trāiciō, -ere, -iēcī, -iectum, pierce.
transeō, -īre, -iī, -itum, pass, pass into, be transformed into.
tremō, -ere, -uī, tremble.
tremulus, -a, -um, *adj.* trembling, quivering, waving.
trepidō (1), be alarmed, hurried, agitated.
trepidus, -a, -um, *adj.* startled, alarmed.
tridentiger, -erī, *m.* trident-bearer, epithet of Neptune.
tristis, -e, *adj.* gloomy, sad, mournful.

triumphus, -ī, *m.* triumph.
Trōia, -ae, *f.* Troy.
Trōius, -a, -um, *adj.* Trojan.
truncus, -a, -um, *adj.* broken.
tueor (2), *dep.* look, gaze at.
tum, *adv.* then.
tumefactus (*part.* of **tumefaciō**), swollen.
tumidus, -a, -um, *adj.* swelling, angry, violent.
tumulō (1), bury.
tumultus, -ūs, *m.* noise, disturbance, turmoil.
tumulus, -ī, *m.* mound, hill; tomb.
turba, -ae, *f.* crowd, troop.
turbō (1), trouble, distress.
turbo, -inis, *m.* whirlwind, hurricane.
turpis, -e, *adj.* shameful, disgraceful; foul, unsightly.
turris, -is, *f.* tower.
tūs, tūris, *n.* incense.
tūtō, *adv.* safely.
tympanum, -ī, *n.* a kettledrum, tambourine.
tyrannus, -ī, *m.* ruler, sovereign.
Tyrius, -a, -um, *adj.* of Tyre, a Phoenician city, famous for its purple.

ubi, *adv.* and *conj.* where, when.
ūdus, -a, -um, *adj.* wet, dank.
ulciscor, -ī, ultus, *dep.* avenge, punish.
ullus, -a, -um, *adj.* any.
ulna, -ae, *f.* elbow, arm.
ulterius, *comp. adv.* further, longer.
ultrā, *adv.* further, longer.
ululātus, -ūs, *m.* shriek, howl.
umbra, -ae, *f.* shade; ghost.
umbrōsus, -a, -um, *adj.* shady.
ūmeō (2), be moist, wet.
umerus, -ī, *m.* shoulder.
ūmidus, -a, -um, *adj.* wet, damp, dewy.
ūnā, *adv.* together, at the same time.
unda, -ae, *f.* wave, water.
undecimus, -a, -um, *adj.* eleventh.
unguis, -is, *m.* fingernail.
ūnicolor, -ōris, *adj.* all of one colour.
ūnus, -a, -um, *adj.* one, alone.
urgeō, -ēre, ursī, press on.
urna, -ae, *f.* (funerary) urn.
ūrō, -ere, ussī, ustum, burn, parch.

usquam, *adv.* anywhere.
uterque, utraque, utrumque, *pron.* either, both.
ūtilis, -e, *adj.* useful, profitable, fitting.
utinam, *adv.* O that!
ūtor, -ī, ūsus, *dep.* use; experience.
utrimque, *adv.* on both sides.

vacō (1), be without.
vacuus, -a, -um, *adj.* empty, abandoned.
vādō (3), go.
vagor (1), *dep.* wander, range.
vagus, -a, -um, *adj.* wandering; uncertain, vague.
valē, *imperative* of **valeō,** farewell.
valenter, *adv.* strongly, violently; *compar.* **valentius.**
vallis, -is, *f.* valley.
vānus, -a, -um, *adj.* empty, shadowy; false, fickle.
variō (1), change.
varius, -a, -um, *adj.* diverse, various.
vastātor, -ōris, *m.* destroyer, ravager.
vastē, *adv.* mightily, terribly; *compar.* **vastius.**
vastus, -a, -um, *adj.* huge, prodigious.
vātes, -is, *m.* priest, prophet; bard, poet.
-ve, *enclitic conj.* or, either.
vehō, -ere, vexī, vectum, carry; *in pass.* ride, fly, go.
vel, *conj.* or, either.
vēlāmen, -inis, *n.* covering, coverlet, mantle.
vēlāmentum, -ī, *n.* an olive branch wreathed with bands of wool.
vellus, -eris, *n.* hide, skin.
vēlō (1), cover, hide.
vēlōciter, *adv.* quickly.
vēlox, -ōcis, *adj.* swift.
vēlum, -ī, *n.* sail.
velut, veluti, *conj.* as, as if.
vēna, -ae, *f.* vein (of ore, 144).
venia, -ae, *f.* pardon.
veniō, -īre, vēnī, ventum, come, resort.
venter, -tris, *m.* womb, fruit of the womb.
ventus, -ī, *m.* wind.
venus, veneris, *f.* love.
verbum, -ī, *n.* word.
vērō, *adv.* indeed.
verrō, -ere, verrī, versum, sweep.
versūtus, -a, -um, *adj.* cunning.
vertex, -icis, *m.* top, summit.

vertīgo, -inis, *f.* eddying, swirling.
vertō, -ere, vertī, versum, turn, change; estrange; *pass.* turn.
vērum, *conj.* but.
vērus, -a, -um, *adj.* true, real.
vestīgium, -iī, *n.* track, footprint.
vestis, -is, *f.* dress, robe.
vetō, -āre, -uī, -itum, forbid.
vetus, -eris, *adj.* old.
vetustus, -a, -um, *adj.* old, ancient.
vexō (1), harass, attack.
via, -ae, *f.* way, path, journey.
vīcīnus, -a, -um, *adj.* near, neighbouring.
vicis, *f. gen.* (no *nom.*), change.
victrix, -icis, *f.* victress; as *adj.* victorious, triumphant.
videō, -ēre, vīdī, vīsum, see; *pass.* seem.
vigil, -ilis, *adj.* wakeful, alert.
villus, -ī, *m.* tuft, hair.
vinciō, -īre, vinxī, vinctum, bind; wreathe, encircle.
vincō, -ere, vīcī, victum, conquer, overcome; surpass.
vinculum, -ī, *n.* bond, fetter.
vindicō (1), rescue, deliver.
vīnētum, -ī, *n.* vineyard.
vīnum, -ī, *n.* wine.
violentus, -a, -um, *adj.* violent.
vir, virī, *m.* man.
vireō (2), be green.
vīres, -ium, *f. pl.* strength.
virga, -ae, *f.* twig, wand.
virgineus, -a, -um, *adj.* of a maiden.
virgo, -inis, *f.* maiden.
virtūs, -tūtis, *f.* valour.
vīrus, -ī, *n.* poison, venom.
vīs, vīm, vī, *f.* strength, force, potency, violence.
vīsō, visere, go to see, visit.
vīta, -ae, *f.* life.
vīvō, -ere, vixī, victum, live.
vīx, *adv.* scarcely.
vocālis, -e, *adj.* tuneful, melodious.
vocō (1), call, summon.
volō (1), fly.
volō, velle, voluī, wish.
volucris, -is, *f.* bird.
vōmer, -eris, *n.* ploughshare.
vōtum, -ī, *n.* vow, prayer, wish.

voveō, -ēre, vōvī, vōtum, vow, promise something to a god; wish for, pray for.

vox, vōcis, *f.* voice.

vulgus, -ī, *n.* common people.

vulnerō (1), wound.

vulnus, -eris, *n.* wound.

vultus, -ūs, *m.* face, features; look, regard.

CPSIA information can be obtained
at www.ICGtesting.com
Printed in the USA
LVHW010745180722
723737LV00008B/257

9 780906 515402